WHAT THEY'R

C000134280

OVER
WHELMED

I thought I was the only one. *Overwhelmed* was the one book that not only made me feel like I wasn't thrown out with the trash as a Christian going through a divorce, but it also gave me practical tools on how to live the single mom life with dignity and honor for God.

—Amanda Carroll, national radio personality formerly with KLOVE, KSBJ, and WGTS, Rocklin, California

As the daughter of a single mom, I have never met a woman more passionate about making sure no mom walks alone... Jennifer Barnes Maggio does an impeccable job providing "real life help". She is making sure the voice of the single mom is heard throughout this nation!

—Tomekia Williams, lead pastor of Catalyst Church, Savannah, Georgia

Moving from overwhelmed to over-comer, Jennifer Maggio writes with the empathy of someone who has been a single mom in the most rugged circumstances. Her clear message is that single motherhood is not your address but your launching pad.

—Peggy Sue Wells, bestselling author *Rediscovering Your Happily Ever After,* Roanoke, Indiana

Our church has been blessed by Jennifer Maggio, her family, and her ministry to single moms. Because she has walked in their shoes before, she is able to speak to the hearts of hurting women. *Overwhelmed* is a must read!

—Mike Haman, Lead Pastor of Healing Place Church in Baton Rouge, Louisiana, and author of *The Second Mile*

Being a single mom is hard. I never dreamed that I would be raising my children alone. Jennifer is brave enough to share her story: the good, the bad, and the ugly. She is open and honest and an encouragement to single moms everywhere. I see myself in the pages of this book.

—LaToya Edwards, Life Coach and author of *Beautifully Broken: Finding God's Purpose in the Pain,* St. Petersburg, Florida

Jennifer Maggio brings together transparency and honesty to reveal true redemption to anyone who has been a victim of abuse.

—Paige Becnel, founder of Blending A
Family Ministry, Castle Rock, Colorado

Overwhelmed literally brought me to tears! Jennifer's story gives us a clear-cut picture that no matter how far down the wrong path we may have ventured, God can and will provide us with that "life abundantly" that only he can so graciously provide.

—Matt Haviland, Founder and President of A Father's
Walk, single dad's ministry, Grand Rapids, Michigan

Jennifer Maggio is a life transformed. She could have resigned to be just another statistic. She is a display of grace and mercy through the transformation of Jesus Christ. Hers is a voice that needs to be heard. She represents Christ to wounded souls everywhere.

—Dino Rizzo, author of *Servolution*,
Birmingham, Alabama

As a single mom, this book was exactly what I was looking for. It is a MUST HAVE for all single parents. Jennifer's openness about her upbringing is gripping, raw and real. I couldn't put it down.

—Janelle Reed, Founder, SingleMomzRock,
Ozark, Missouri

Overwhelmed is a poignant and powerful story of the transformative power of the grace of God in the midst of heartache, pain, and loss. Jennifer Maggio's passion for Jesus and love for people will encourage and inspire you to not just survive life but thrive.

—Mercy Lokulutu, Pastor, Speaker, and author
of As You Wish, Riviera Beach, Maryland

OVER WHELMED

OVER WHELMED

the life of a single mom

THIRD EDITION

Published by TLSM Publishing
Baton Rouge, Louisiana | 225.341.8055
www.thelifeofasinglemom.com

Book design copyright © 2017 by TLSM Publishing. All rights reserved. Cover design by Kedra Deggins

Published in the United States of America

ISBN: 9798675341511

DEDICATION

To my husband, Jeff, who stood by me and supported the dream of working with single mothers, even when it did not make sense. You are the light of my life. You are my life partner. I love you.

To my awesome, wonderful children. Much of my life's work has been dedicated to the betterment of your life. You are all my heart, my world. I adore you and cannot wait to see what each of you becomes. I love you.

To the Chapman and Dean Families, thank you for always being there.

To my twin, who has loved me through thick and thin.

To my countless friends, family, and mentors that have read the book, offered their opinions, and been a listening ear through nights of frustration and stress. Thank you.

TABLE OF CONTENTS

PART ONE: THE STORY

PART TWO: VICTORY IS WON!

PART THREE: EQUIPPING LEADERS

PART ONE

THE STORY

PREFACE

As I combed through the shelves of the bookstores, libraries, and pages upon pages of numerous Internet sites, I could hardly find anything on the single parenting experience. There is even less written from a Christian perspective. Some will read this book out of curiosity. Perhaps the cover or the title caught your eye. Others will pick it up out of sheer desperation, because you cannot take it another second. The journey is too long and too hard. You are tired. You are looking for help. You might be thinking, "Maybe this chick will have something to say that can help me get through this almost unbearable time in my life."

Maybe you married well and had a picture perfect life, but woke up one morning and it all seemed to vanish. The divorce caused your whole world to fall apart. There are others who are widows or young teen moms.

There are also moms out there who don't know who the father of their child is. And there are many moms who have not seen their child's father since conception. Whoever you are, single mom, this was written for you.

There is a passion burning deep within me that I can barely contain; a passion to see every single mom realize that she can make it, that her beginning is not her ending. I want to be real and raw.

This is a journey through my life and what I learned about survival, about myself, and most importantly about my heavenly Father. I hope you pick up some tips of survival through these next few pages. I hope you find you are stronger than you thought.

CHAPTER 1

IN THE BEGINNING

When I was three years old, I awoke late one night to some type of commotion in the kitchen. With my favorite blanket in tow, I stumbled down the hall, half-asleep into a scene that I will never forget. I was horrified to see my dad leaning over the kitchen sink while my step mom and sister-in-law leaned over him washing blood from his head and face. I stood there shocked as they cried and scrubbed him clean. At some point, I was noticed and quickly ushered back to bed. I didn't know what to think of all this. I lay in bed that night scared and confused fearing my dad may not be alive when I awakened the next morning. I cried myself to sleep wondering what had happened to my daddy. I later learned that my dad had driven his 1978 Chevrolet Silverado into a large ravine that night, yet somehow managed to get it out and drive home. The windshield was crushed. The truck was dented. My step mom stitched his head at home to avoid questioning from authorities. He was driving drunk. This was my earliest memory of my dad. In those early years, it was rare that I saw him without a Miller Little Pony (beer) in his hand.

My daddy was raised an honest, hard-working farmer in a family with six children. His parents married at fifteen years old. They raised chickens and pigs and grew their own vegetables. They worked from sun-up to sun-down. My daddy really did miss the first few weeks of school every year due to picking cotton! His mother made all of his clothes by hand and washed them with a washboard. They didn't have electricity and used coal oil lanterns for many years for lighting at night. They had no indoor plumbing and, therefore, used an outhouse. Many years after indoor plumbing was installed, I remember my grandmother still using the outhouse. Old habits die hard, I guess.

Growing up, my dad's family churned their own butter. They killed and cooked their own pigs. They hunted deer and turkey and fished at the local ponds. Trips to town were rare and only made when absolutely necessary. Times were hard. My dad was raised on country music and gospel hymns by a tobacco-chewing daddy and a thick-skinned Mississippi momma. It was simple living. He grew up in the fields working and playing until dark. He eventually grew to love basketball and became quite good at it. He worked hard with his grades and was offered basketball scholarships to go to college after his high school graduation, but he chose the United States Army instead. He spent a couple years in the army and later married his high school sweetheart. They raised two sons together, but they divorced after almost twenty years of marriage. Both of his sons were born with heart problems. One had major surgery as a young man, and the other had a heart-related condition.

My dad knew this son was dying and lay awake at night and watched his son's heart beat up and down in his chest, fearing that any night would be his last. I cannot imagine what this does to a parent, to watch their child die before their eyes, but my brother did die after a long battle with his heart at only seventeen years old. This crushed my dad emotionally, and he turned to drinking (and eventually to women) to solve his problems. He was a full-scale alcoholic by the time I was born. He had also been a very active deacon in the church, but he completely fell away from any activity associated with the church after his son died.

My daddy already had a lifetime of disappointments before I was ever born; a failed marriage, the death of his son, the death of his baby brother a few years prior, and disappointments through his local church, and I do not believe he ever fully recovered from them.

He met and married my mother a few years after his son died. I was born shortly after in 1977, along with a twin sister, in a rural Mississippi town, not far from where my dad was raised. I do not know much about my parent's relationship, other than my daddy's drinking interfered with it. I know that my dad was violent with her, and my mom was unhappy. Their relationship was a roller coaster of extreme emotions, either ultimate bliss or utter turmoil. My mom was exhausted from it all. She eventually began to turn her heart back toward the things of God, where she had found comfort in her childhood. She actively attended church with my sister and me. She began to play the piano for the local church. She longed for my dad to be part of her church family, but the hurt from his past kept him away.

One Sunday in November 1978, my daddy had gone deer hunting, as he did most every weekend during hunting season. There was lots more beer drinking than hunting going on during these trips. My mother got us dressed as usual and rushed out the door for church. She loaded us in our car seats and we began the short trek . Our church was less than five miles down the road. Out of nowhere, a teenage drunk driver slammed us into a tree, less than a mile from our own home. My mother was killed instantly. My dad heard on the radio that there was an accident with fatalities on the street where we lived. He knew that his wife had been killed. My twin sister and I suffered major bruising, cuts, and scarring. We were unable to walk for months after the event. Neighbors, friends, and family rallied around to help care for us as my daddy dealt with his grief.

The shock of my mother's death hit the whole family hard. The young, beautiful Sammye was gone. What would happen to her twin babies? Her whole life had been ahead of her. She was but thirty-two years old. We had family from all over the country arrive for her funeral. There were plenty of pictures taken that night to put in an album for us when we were old enough to understand.

I looked through that photo album many times growing up, wondering how my life would have been different with my mother living.

It seemed that almost by daybreak my dad had remarried again, wife number three was named Barbara. My dad worked offshore as a drill man for an oil company, which meant that he worked away from home a week at a time. I remember a conversation that I had with my dad years later about his third marriage. He confessed to me that he married Barbara as a babysitter for my twin sister and me, as he still needed to provide a living for us after my mom was gone. I remember very little about Barbara. I do, however, remember that her forms of punishment were cruel. She locked us in a closet for extended periods of time. When Daddy was away at work, she would not feed us regularly. She beat us for disobeying, even as toddlers. As quickly as she came into the family, she was gone. I do not know why.

In my family, there was kind of a code of silence. No one was asking my dad why he felt the need to marry over and over again. No one dealt with the alcoholism. Whether it was through shame or some sick loyalty, I cannot say. All that is for certain is in a world of double names like Nannie Lou, Mary Alice, and Louisa Mae, you knew that someone would knock you in the head if you aired too much dirty laundry. That's just the way things were in those days. All my southern country girls know what I'm talking about. There is something about a wide-waisted Mississippi woman in an apron with a wet dishtowel that you just don't mess with. You learn to accept your world as normal.

When Daddy married wife number four, we were pretty used to the idea of our home being a revolving door with people coming and going regularly. We called each wife "Momma," as we were told to do, and didn't speak of our own mother very often. Our new Momma, Francis, came with a teenage son. By the time I was three years old, my stepbrother was regularly molesting me while he allowed onlookers to watch. I never discussed any of this. It would be many years before I learned that this sort of thing was not normal and many years after that before I ever discussed it aloud.

Daddy and "Momma" would go out to dinner and leave us under the supervision of the neighbors next door. They had an older son, who also molested me. We would be sent next door to play with him many, many times through those next few years. As a child, I cannot tell you exactly how I felt about all of this. I have only been able to remember bits and pieces of that period in my life. I remember more bad than good, unfortunately. My dad was gone quite a bit with work and molestation became common at the hands of many in my life.

There were later problems in this marriage, too. Infidelity was involved. I was brought to my dad's friends homes, all of which were women, to stay the night. We stayed up watching rated R movies at four years old, while Dad and his lady friends visited in the bedroom.

Momma Francis had her own problems. She rolled marijuana and smoked it regularly with her friends in front of me. She had some extra-curricular activities of her own, not the least of which was sleeping with someone in our own home that I walked in on, while my dad was at work. They divorced shortly thereafter.

As I said earlier, my dad had a drinking problem. This coupled with a bad temper and multiple divorces led to some rocky nights in my home. He would come home drunk and tear up the whole house, destroying lamps, pictures, chairs, and anything else in his way. He screamed violently for hours on end. He would cry and kick chairs. He would abuse different women in his life. He drove home drunk many times, including straight through our front yard. He made large circles over and over again with his truck on our lawn, honking and screaming, all the while. To a young girl this was a terrifying life.

My dad was an angry drunk. When he consumed alcohol, he became mean and violent. Anyone who wronged him would hear about it in his drunken frenzies. This was no different the night he stood at the end of our driveway with pistol in hand as he screamed obscenities at my uncle across the street. My uncle, in turn, stood at the end of his driveway screaming back with his pistol in tow. This standoff lasted for some time as I watched through my bedroom window, fearing my daddy would be killed. Most of the time he didn't remember any of it the next morning, and I daily pretended it never happened. By the time wife number five came around, he drank until he passed out regularly.

There was never a period of more than a few weeks when a woman didn't live in our home. So it was no surprise when Candy showed up, wife number five. That is when the adventure really began. My dad adored her. She was twenty years his junior. She had three children of her own, which made a total of five children in our home, all roughly the same age.

During their marriage, I was somewhere between nine and twelve years old. The next few years ran together. My dad changed jobs several times, but always stayed away from home working for extended periods of time. This left us home alone with Candy. In her youth, Candy had gone through some brushes with the law and was on probation most of their marriage. Her own children had been living with their grandparents. When she married my dad, she took on five children and was learning how to raise us effectively. She failed miserably. There was something deeply disturbing about her parenting style. She was very child-like and oftentimes treated us like her mental equivalents and not her children.

Candy had an eight-year-old son who was mentally handicapped. When she married my dad, her son had been living in a special facility for the mentally impaired. We retrieved him from the facility soon after they married. Candy was in no way prepared for the responsibility of caring for him. My stepsisters and I, aged nine to eleven, took turns feeding him, changing his dirty diapers, and often bathing him. I was never bitter about caring for him, because I loved him very much, but I now look back and think it was inappropriate for pre-adolescent girls to constantly view and clean genitalia of a same-aged boy. In addition, the responsibility of caring for a mentally-challenged individual should be left to parents and professionals, not little girls.

I was only ten years old when Candy first brought pornography into our home. She had stolen the videos from a local video store. She began playing those in front of us. At such a young age, I was infiltrated with thoughts and images that no child should experience. I remember her laughing vividly as we hid our faces in shame. Theft, dishonesty, pornography, and infidelity were all a common part of those years with her. As children, she would drive us around at night, and we would be asked to steal newspapers from the yards of neighbors rather than get our own subscription. We would take yard art from the yards. She wrote insufficient checks all over town. She even stole my dead mother's wedding ring from a picture album and pawned it for money.

Candy tortured me in many ways. As a joke, she would chase us around the house with a cup that was filled with her own feces. She would sit on us and restrain us, while spitting in our faces. She was an obese woman who sat on top of me topless, while simultaneously slapping me in the face repeatedly with her large breasts, as she laughed hysterically. She beat me with the belt many times. She slapped me in the face many times. She screamed that she hated me and threatened me once. She slammed me against the wall and choked me until I felt I was going to die. She wanted to bully me. She loved us one day and hated us the next. It was terrifying.

One of the other normalcies of the time was to spend the night with Candy's parents, our step-grandparents. They would let me play outside for hours after dark on the trampoline and prepare my favorite meal for dinner, macaroni and cheese. They hugged me and doted on me. They let me drive the riding lawn mower. They did all the things grandparents were supposed to do. At night, my cousins and I took turns sleeping with grandma and grandpa, because they slept in separate beds. Grandpa began inappropriate behavior with me almost immediately. I never told a living soul. I was scared no one would believe me.

Through all that, I loved Candy. She was my mom for that short while. I had no mother. I wanted so desperately to be loved. There were normal times during all the turmoil, where we went to church as a family and had Sunday dinner afterwards. We had big family Thanksgivings and Christmases with extended family. We had large family gatherings that would last for hours. I cherished those times. I needed that normalcy, even if it was only pretend and only temporary.

CHAPTER 2

CHILDHOOD

Infidelity crept into my dad's marriage to Candy also. They soon divorced. Through the years my dad had many girlfriends and wives. At this point, you may be questioning why he did some of the things he did. Why did he make some of the decisions he did? Why didn't he protect me? Don't. It's a fruitless thought-process that won't bring you any closer to the answers than I am today. All I know is that when people are hurting, they do strange things. I let go of wondering "Why?" a long time ago.

The divorce from Candy was very ugly. There was lots of fighting over money, who was going to get the bedroom furniture, the pots and pans, the end table. Everything was an argument.

In the days leading up to the divorce, Daddy loaded us in the car at night and we drove around looking for Candy to see what she was up to, driving from bar to bar until the wee hours of the morning. The whole thing seemed to drag on forever. The day the divorce was official, I was so relieved that I would never live with her again. Yet, in some way, I was sad; sad that yet another mother was gone.

Not long after Candy left, at only twelve years old, I began feeling pressure to have sex. Part of the pressure was that I hung around with people much older than I was at the time. The other part was pressure I put on myself because I wanted to be liked, valued, and to fit in with the cool kids. We spent many hours on the weekends driving around aimlessly from one teen hangout to another. We drank alcohol most every weekend. My dad never noticed that I came home drunk, repeatedly. The episodes had gotten so bad that there were times I couldn't remember anything about the night before. Daddy was preoccupied with his own life and dating.

I put off the pressure of having sex until I was thirteen. I had avoided it as long as I thought I could, and since I was dating a sixteen-year-old, I just did it. We drove several miles in the middle of nowhere and it happened. That night in a field in no man's land, I thought so little of myself that I gave away one of the most precious gifts my heavenly Father gave me. It was over in a matter of minutes and I felt sick. I knew he didn't love me. What had I done? I didn't tell anyone, but it wasn't long before my entire circle of friends and his friends knew. I was embarrassed and ashamed. The guy barely spoke to me afterwards.

My dad was oblivious to my new lifestyle of drinking and sex. I jumped from one short relationship to another, each with a similar story, only to have my heart broken over and over again. The guys didn't call me afterwards. Most of them were many years older than me. Oftentimes, I just became another face in the crowd, another notch on someone's belt.

The next eighteen months of my life were that way. I battled back and forth with what I was doing. I wasn't happy. I wanted to stop this cycle of emotional turmoil, but I couldn't. It saddens me to even think upon those things now. I was so lost, lonely, and hurting. I needed someone to love me. There was so much abandonment in my past. As soon as one boy would show me attention, I latched onto it. Half of the time, I didn't even feel bad about it. I almost thought of it as survival, a means of masking how I really felt. I felt the call of God on my life, on the one hand. On the other hand, I felt certain that he didn't know what my life was like. He didn't know the things I had to endure. Certainly, no one in that church knew of the things that went on behind closed doors at my house.

You see, I had been attending church all my life. My dad didn't usually attend with us. He would drive up to the front door, drop us off, and leave. I felt embarrassed when I saw normal families all sitting together. I thought my family was weird, and I was pretty sure everyone else did, too.

At nine years old, at the prompting of the pastor's invitation, I accepted Jesus into my heart. I was so excited and full of joy. I began to read my Bible daily and prayed regularly. I was baptized the following Sunday. It was a big day. The next couple of years, I became very close with God. I attended church three times weekly. Even with all the abuse I suffered, I still committed to being at church.

I made several good church friends. I did enjoy hanging out with their families. It gave me a sense of belonging. There was something great about being with genuinely good girls that came from good families that loved the Lord. It was peaceful and they always made me feel welcome.

But slowly, I began to slip away from those friends and the church. The distractions from home were too much. My stepmom made fun of me for being a goody-two-shoe who thought I was better than everyone else. Her behavior, along with my newfound interest in boys, made me put the Lord on the back burner. That's where I kept him for many years thereafter. And that's where I found myself, away from God, entering one lonely relationship after another.

During this tumultuous time, my dad brought home Mary. Mary was in her forties with bleached blond hair. She wore heavy blue eye make-up and long artificial fingernails. She reminded me a great deal of Tammy Faye Baker in appearance. Although she smiled and spoke kindly to me, there was something about her that made me very uncomfortable. One of the first things she told me after we met was that she wanted to be friends and hoped I would learn to confide in her. I believed her for about thirty seconds.

Two months later, she became wife number six. She and Daddy were married in a small ceremony at our home with a small gathering of friends and family present. We decorated their car for their honeymoon. We threw rice on them as they jumped in the car and drove away. I wondered, as I waved, how long this one would last. I can't say that I cared one way or another.

Mary was the first wife since my own mother's death that I did not call "Momma." I was fourteen by now and had had just about enough of all that. My attitude reflected as much, too. Mary had three adult children that had been raised by her ex-husband, so she had very little parenting experience. From day one, I emphatically believe that she resented that my dad had twin teenage daughters still living at home. She hoped we would disappear, and when we didn't, it became her mission to hate us. She was very successful at it.

At first, things seemed fairly normal. Daddy and Mary did their own thing as newlyweds. They went to dinner and watched movies. They visited with friends. My dad had a very strict persona, in that boys weren't allowed to call our home or come over. But the truth is, I had very little supervision and I took full advantage of it. I ran from one thing to another. I had sleepovers with whomever I wished. I sneaked out of the house. I sneaked boys over after dark.

Is it any wonder that at thirteen years old, I began to have sex?

In this desperate need to be loved, I was Miss Perfectionist. I was the classic over-achiever. I was a straight A student. I was class president. I was a member of the Library Club, the Fellowship of Christian Athletes, and the Beta Club. I was on the homecoming court and in Sweetheart Pageants. I was a peer counselor. I was the one chosen to give all the speeches and opening prayers at school assemblies. Any honor that I could have possibly won, I fought hard to win it. At least in that moment, I was on top of the world. I felt respected. I felt loved.

It seemed that no matter how hard I worked, it was never good enough, though. I had teachers, coaches, and counselors that encouraged me through the years, but not my dad. And I even think my dad bragged about me to friends and family, but he rarely told me that he was proud of me. He never gave me a big hug and told me to never settle for less than God's best. He didn't tell me I was a princess that was waiting on just the right prince. I didn't feel loved by my dad or stepmom at the time.

My twin sister and I were announced covaledictorians only days before the annual baccalaureate service. It happened to be held on the Sunday morning of Mother's Day. As a tribute to mothers, our school decided to have each graduate's mother sit with them during the high school baccalaureate service. At some point in the ceremony, we would hand a red rose to our mother. Because our biological mother was deceased, it was expected that my stepmother would accompany us to the event. However, she did not, nor did my dad. So as not to sit alone, we had two kind teachers to volunteer to sit with us.

I had obtained the highest honor bestowed upon a graduating senior, and still, it was not good enough. I was hurt and humiliated. Daddy was a man's man who was raised to not express much emotion. It was not masculine. I consequently grew up with very little affection. I loved my dad more than I can express. For nineteen years, he and my twin sister were the only two constants in my life. No matter how many mistakes I made, he was still my dad. I loved him, but I just couldn't talk to him. I sat beside him on our front porch in silence dozens of times through my teenage years. I wanted to talk to him so desperately. A thousand thoughts roamed through my mind, questions I wanted to ask, but I couldn't. I just couldn't.

His current wife was no better. Mary had expressed her desire to get to know my sister and me in the first few weeks of the marriage. Those feelings soon dissipated, and she became what I later referred to as "the evil stepmother." From all the stepmoms we had, I thought she was the most abusive. All the other's abuses were blatant, out there in plain view. But Mary's abuse was much more secretive and calculating.

Not any one incident made her abusive. It was the culmination of many events. My dad worked away from home, so again, I was left with a stepmother to watch after me. She didn't treat me the same when Daddy was around as when he was gone. When he was away, she would stop by a restaurant on the way home from work and pick up dinner only for herself. She brought it in, went to her bedroom, locked the door, and ate it. When she did this, I began to cook dinner in the kitchen. She would then come from her room screaming at me for messing up the dishes. This was a frequent occurrence. When our dad was home, however, she bought enough for the whole family.

She also bought new clothes for herself three to four times weekly. Never did she buy anything for us, not even a shirt. However, I was required to wash all her clothes separate from the rest of the family, "Because your clothes will mess up my clothes," she would say. She bought a few things for Daddy from time to time, but she pretended I did not exist except to be rude and spiteful.

Unbeknown to my dad, she ultimately began recording all phone conversations coming into and out of our home. She recorded each call and later listened to them. Why? Had I gotten involved with drugs? Was I engaged in some illegal activity? No. This was a way to control and manipulate me, and ultimately to embarrass me. The phone recordings went on for two years.

Like every wife before, she came into the family insisting we went to church on Sundays. We did this for a brief time, until I would mess up. If I was disobedient in any way, she began to scream that I wasn't a Christian and the whole church thing was a farce that she wasn't going to participate in anymore. She once made me sit down with the pastor, a man I barely knew, for counseling. Why wouldn't my own parents sit down and talk to me? Couldn't my dad see that I was hurting?

There were moments in my junior high and high school years that were genuinely happy. I did a great job of masking all the ugly underneath. I enjoyed the spotlight. I enjoyed my Daddy giving me a big hug and telling me he was proud of me, however rare that moment was. I liked that people thought I was smart. It somehow gave me value. It made me hang on to every future relationship with a boy for far too long. If any boy was smooth enough to throw compliments my way...I clung for dear life.

CHAPTER 3

AND SO IT GOES

At the age of fourteen, there was not one thing, I didn't already know about life. Seemingly, I had it all figured out. I was young and carefree. My parents were just plain, old, and dumb, in my opinion. Besides, they didn't know what it was like to be my age.

As I finished up my first year of high school, I could hardly wait for the summer. There would be slumber parties and prank phone calls. There would be no homework and no bedtimes. And there would be boys—new boys, old boys, new crushes, old flames. Oh, the joy of adolescence!

As with most teens, my friends and I hung out almost every day during the summer. We did typical teenage girl things. We sunbathed, read magazines, listened to The New Kids on the Block on the radio, and made fun of our parents. We giggled and squealed as we told each other silly stories. We called boys, hung up, and called them back again.

We also spent a great deal of time at my friend Jenn's house. There was one major reason for this. She lived in a fairly large neighborhood, much bigger than any of ours. This was important, because it meant more potential to bump into boys. If you don't realize how important that is, then you have forgotten about being fourteen! We would all rush over in the afternoon and spend hours styling our hair and applying makeup. We then went walking up and down every street in the neighborhood laughing, talking, and singing; anything to be noticed. We almost always bumped into boys that we could ignore.

I also enjoyed spending time at Jenn's house because it was always so warm and inviting. Her mom was one of those moms that you could talk to about anything and she wouldn't freak out on you. I found that comforting. Jenn was the friend that made the biggest impression on me in my early years about serving God. She was always at church, always smiling. I do not remember us talking much about church or God in our teenage years, but her actions spoke louder than her words.

But, by far, the most fun we had that summer were the evening hangouts at the mall. Every Friday and Saturday night, the local mall was the place to be for teens.

Now, we did not have permission to go to the mall. I'm not sure why we didn't have permission to go there, other than there would be boys at the mall and they were all standing outside. Yep—outside. They would stare at us as we walked by, and my dad did not like that idea. He did, however, see no problem with us going to the local bowling alley, infested with smoke and forty-year old drunken men with beards and rotten teeth, since it was inside. The logic here escapes me. But this situation presented a dilemma. I mean, all the cool kids were at the mall, so we could not possibly hang out at the bowling alley all night.

The mall was strategically located directly across the highway from the bowling alley. So, we did what any normal fourteen year olds (with a sense of rebellious adventure) would do. After being driven to the bowling alley, we waited thirty seconds for our parents to get out of sight, and we headed across the highway.

We did this several dozen times that summer. It may occur to you at this point that crossing a busy four-lane highway in the dark with traffic going upwards at sixty miles per hour isn't such a good idea. However, we had already discussed it and decided any risk of bodily harm was worth it to get to the mall. I told you I had life figured out. I was practically an adult.

Then, came the fateful day of the accident. We all decided to cross the highway, as we had done many times before. We were running late so we had to hurry. As I approached the median, I ran over the grass, tripped and fell, twisting my ankle on the way down. My friends had already crossed the road. They screamed back at me to hurry. "Get up!" they yelled, not realizing my ankle was twisted. In what seemed like an eternity, although I am certain it was more like ten seconds, I lay in the grass with cars whizzing by at speeds above sixty miles per hour. I screamed, "Go on without me...me...me! I'll be fine...fine...fine!"

As adults, we have laughed many times about how dramatic we were that night. And yes, I did get up and limp over to the mall that night. Summer always lent itself to happy memories for me, like the time my friend slipped on a piece of barbecue chicken, fell down, and her plate knocked her unconscious (Yes, it's the truth!), or the time I busted my shoe open during a friendly game of kickball. I had to wear the ruined shoe the rest of the day while my foot slipped in and out. Summer always allowed me to be in a different place mentally, a happy place. Reality was whatever I wanted it to be. It allowed me to escape, briefly from the hell that went on behind closed doors at home.

The summer of my freshman year of high school also started a new adventure in my life, high school basketball. I went to my first summer basketball camp. I walked onto the gym floor with a group of kids that I knew were superior to me in athletic skill and ability. But, there I was. I was going for it. After years of prodding from my dad, I walked onto the floor for the first time to play high school basketball. I didn't care much for the sport, actually, but oh, how my daddy did! I would listen to him talk about his glory days when he was leading point guard of his high school and had been offered basketball scholarships around the state. And so began my basketball career on that hot summer day.

There were forty or so boys and girls in the gym. The whistle blew and we ran, and ran, and ran. We did dribbling drills, lay ups, free throws, and jump shots. And we ran and ran and then, ran some more. The whole practice lasted about three hours. It was a blur. I was dizzy and near fainting, I'm sure. My face was beet-red and sweaty. My long ponytail flopped around and stuck to my sweaty face as I practically crawled to the water fountain outside the gym.

I noticed a tall boy standing with a group of other kids waiting in line to get water, too. I knew him from school. Well, that's to say, I knew his name. He was a basketball player for our high school team. We had had some classes together through junior high school and I knew him as a class clown but today, he looked kind of different, and kind of cute.

My turn came up at the water fountain. I couldn't help but notice that he watched me as I walked away. *This could get interesting,* I thought to myself, as I walked away trying to be as attractive as possible with a red sweaty face. I began to wonder if he had a girlfriend and what he was like. I knew he was a great athlete, as anyone could tell, but what else was there to know about this guy? Maybe I would just have to find out.

My dad was born in 1935 in rural Mississippi where he picked cotton, tended a farm, and used an outhouse. In Mississippi during those days, there was a well-defined clear line between blacks and whites, sadly. I pause to mention this for only one reason. That tall, dark, handsome basketball player that I met during basketball camp was literally just that! He was black. It would mean very little to most of you today, but coming from a conservative, traditional, older father who was born in rural Mississippi in the 1930s, this fact would prove to be a big deal -- and yet one more reason why I was intrigued.

I completed that long week of basketball camp, running and sweating all the while. The boy and I innocently flirted throughout the week, tossing each other quick glances or smiles, or conveniently getting into the same drill lines. I found myself thinking of him throughout the week. Of course, I thought about quite a few boys that summer. I mean, I was fourteen, after all.

I didn't see the boy for the rest of the summer. I went on with my summer plans, visiting relatives, swimming with friends, sleepovers, the whole nine. In fact, I didn't think about him again until several months later.

In August, I began my sophomore year of high school and the anticipation of a new school year. You lie awake at night thinking of the first day of school. Who will my teachers be? Will the classes be hard? Will my friends be in my class? Will there be any new boys at school? I began classes that hot August day, and there he was, Mr. Basketball Boy, also known as Dillon. We did have classes together. We began to talk a little at a time. We would share notes or smile. We then moved on to sitting together at basketball games. There's something exciting about young love, about the newness of a new relationship. What began as innocent flirting turned into a full-blown romance that year.

However, the seven years that followed were anything but romantic.

CHAPTER 4

THE RELATIONSHIP

Although I tried to hide it, it didn't take long for my dad to find out about Dillon. One night, the two of us had decided that Dillon would come over to my house and spend some time, as he had done many times before. My sister and dad had gone to the local high school football game. I chose to stay home. Dillon came over at around eight o'clock that night. I pretended to go to sleep because my stepmom, Mary, was home. She came in the other end of the house and walked in the bedroom. I was so surprised to see her that I began to fumble my words. She immediately caught on that something was wrong. She saw Dillon lying on the floor on the other side of the bed. I was horrified. I had been caught. I was no longer Daddy's perfect princess. Mary called my dad at the game that night. They called the cops. I didn't want to disappoint my dad, but I wasn't sorry. I loved Dillon. I almost instantly began to think about how I would continue to see him. We would just have to be more creative.

It seems that that incident only made it more exciting to sneak him over. It only fueled my passion and love for him. Slowly, I told my friends one by one. The news traveled through the school like wildfire. Many friends were no longer my friends because they disapproved of me liking someone who was black. I began to feel more isolated making the relationship with him even more important for me to hold on to.

Did I mention that Dillon had a girlfriend? Yep. He hung with her most days at school, holding hands, and pretending everything was okay. I just walked around and pretended not to notice. I convinced myself that the only reason he wasn't with me was because our parents didn't want us together. In fact, I created this whole Romeo-and-Juliet love story that made me think that all our troubles related to how the world and our families didn't want us together. But once we were adults, we would be together forever. He loved me too, ya know.

I continued this same story in my mind as he began to get more and more and more girlfriends in the years that followed. He wasn't acknowledging our relationship to anyone, although he spent most nights at my house. By the end of our junior year of high school, I had heard of more girlfriends than I even wanted to count. He slept with numerous girls, even my friends. I began to be so hurt, so broken. Yet, there was that part of me that needed him to love me, to hold me. I needed to hear the words that he told me. "You are beautiful." "You are the one I really love." "You are the one I cannot wait to see every day," he would say. I believed every word.

Before I knew it, I had spent three years in a relationship that was so volatile that none of my friends even wanted to hear the stories anymore. I was wrapped up in the drama of arguing with other girls, screaming at Dillon, and terrible phone calls, and I did not even care that the principal and all the teachers knew about it. My reputation was ruined. And it didn't matter. As long as Dillon and I were together, everything would be just fine.

My high school years were filled with these dramatic events that all related to Dillon. When I heard of a new relationship that he was pursuing or a new girlfriend he liked, I would become enraged. *How dare she like him! She knows we are together. She is just trying to mess things up for me. She is just jealous of what we have,* I thought.

I almost always directed my anger toward the other girls, not him. I slapped the girls. I screamed and argued and cussed. I started fights. I wound up in the principal's office more than once. I was in the streets fighting over him with absolutely no dignity whatsoever. I went into hysterics every time I heard the stories. Yet, I still let him come over almost every night. He convinced me time and time again that the rumors were all lies. He constantly told me that he would never love anyone more than me. We would one day be married and live happily ever after. By the time he left my house at night, I was on cloud nine, convinced of his undying love for me, until the cycle started all over again the next day.

I finally graduated high school in 1995. There were approximately four hundred students at the school the year I graduated. There were almost seventy girls pregnant. That's right. It was an epidemic. It was cool to be pregnant. Through my four years of high school, I watched girls one by one become pregnant. I started thinking of what it would be like to have a baby. Would that make Dillon love me even more? Would he leave everyone else so that we could finally start a family? I did not care whether or not I got pregnant. I went on to have two miscarriages before I graduated high school. I hid those very well. My dad never knew. By my senior year of high school, I got pregnant a third time. When I graduated high school, I was named covaledictorian with my twin sister. It was such a proud day to walk across the stage with my twin sister to accept the numerous awards and scholarships.

We both gave valedictory addresses. We received several full-paid scholarships to college. I received more awards that night than I could carry and had to have help loading them in the car after the ceremony. I had everything going for me. Yet it was such a sad day. I knew I wouldn't be going on to college. I knew I had a baby growing inside me. And at seventeen years old, I had no idea what I was going to do.

That night after graduation, I went to Dillon's house. I knew this was the last night I would see him for quite some time, and I needed to spend some time with him. My dad had sold our home, and we were loaded up and moving to another state the next morning. Needless to say, Dillon was not near as sentimental as I was. I cried a great deal that night wondering what my future held, when I would see Dillon again. I moved the next morning and didn't talk to him again for several weeks.

The original plan was to graduate high school, move the next morning, and start college a few months later. However, I asked my dad if I could go visit friends for a few weeks back in our old hometown before college started. I packed my things and hugged my dad tightly, fearing this would be the last time I ever saw him. I was six months pregnant by now, although no one knew. Friends came to pick me up, and we headed back to our hometown, our graduation site.

Although my dad thought I was gone for only a few days, I knew I would never return home. After getting settled at my friend's home, I went to the local free health unit to get my first prenatal care. I began the tedious process of applying for government assistance programs— food stamps, welfare, Medicaid, and government housing. At the end of the two-week visit, I had successfully applied for and was receiving all my assistance, but I still had nowhere to live.

I finally told my dad that I was pregnant. I called him and nervously explained my situation. I cringed and waited for his response. His exact words to me were, "Have a nice life." He kicked me out of my house. My twin sister went away to college and it was the first time we had ever been separated. I was so alone. I had no clothes, no money, no way to provide for my child, nowhere to live, and no plan.

Dillon continued to live at home with his parents that summer and we talked and visited over the next few weeks, but he was more worried about going away to college than my well-being. He talked of playing basketball (because he had earned an athletic scholarship) at his new school. I knew that he was not worried about where I would live or how I would survive, but deep down, I needed him. He was all I had left.

One of my closest friends, Jenn, finally invited me to move in with her and her family (the Chapmans). I was seven months pregnant at the time. I had an aunt in Texas that bought a 1984 Mercury Lynx to help me out. That thing left me on the side of the road at least twice per week and smoked so bad that no one could drive behind me, but I was thankful nonetheless. I spent the night in that car sometimes, partly because I felt I had nowhere to go and partly because I didn't want anyone to know how bad I was hurting.

Becky Chapman, Jenn's mom, and her family allowed me to stay with them as long as I needed to. She was the backbone of that family. She cared for me during those next few months as if I was her own child. She became my mom. She was such a special part of my life during that time. Years later, I continued to buy her Mother's Day gifts. She took me to doctor's appointments. She bought me clothes. She spent hours and hours talking to me. She was my comfort in those many lonely months that followed. I will always be eternally grateful that she took me in, provided me meals and a place to sleep. She tried to make me feel part of her family, but the truth is, I was hurting deep inside, missing my own family. I missed my daddy, the one that had been the only constant in my life for so many years. I missed my twin sister that I had grown up with.

That summer, as Dillon was preparing to go away to college, I had begun to hear rumors of another girlfriend being pregnant. I was devastated. Here I was thinking that we would build a family together and that we could finally be together, but he had other plans. I found out that the rumors were true. He did, in fact, have another baby on the way. I felt like the laughing stock of town. I could barely make myself get out of bed in the mornings. In fact, many times I didn't. I began to contemplate giving my baby up for adoption. I didn't know what to do. I was as alone in the world as I had ever been.

It was about eight o'clock one night when the phone rang. It was a long-time friend from high school on the other end. She said, "Jennifer, did you hear that Dillon was getting married tomorrow?" *What? What was she talking about?* I had seen Dillon earlier that day (because he had not left for college, yet) and had no idea. I began to make phone calls and could not believe my ears! Yes, he was getting married in only a few short hours! *How could this be? I don't understand. How could he do this to me?*

I talked to him on the phone much of that night and through the next morning as he got ready for his own wedding. He claimed that he was being forced to do it, because the girl that was pregnant was so young and her parents were forcing him to marry her. I wanted so desperately to believe that. I convinced myself it was true. I can honestly say that even now that was the darkest hour of my life.

At the very moment that he was marrying someone else across town, I curled into a ball onto the floor and cried and cried. I screamed out in terrible pain and torment. I could not stop screaming. I was on my knees screaming, "Why? Why? Why?" It was the closest I have ever been to suicide. I did not care what my future held.

I did not care about my baby. All I knew was that my life was over. I did not want to go on. I could not face the world with the shame and embarrassment I felt. I could not handle one more phone call asking how I was taking the news. I could not bear one more report of them leaving on their honeymoon. It made me sick. I cried. I hurt. The pain was almost unbearable. I felt that I physically could not get out of the bed. And so I didn't.

I spent the remainder of my pregnancy so depressed that I could barely move. I thought many times of giving my baby up for adoption and killing myself. What reason was there to go on? My family was gone. My friends were mostly gone. I had no money, no future. The one person I had been living for had just married someone else. I had never known pain like that before.

As the next few months passed, Dillon went on to college. He called me and wrote me regularly. He told me how much he really loved only me, how this whole thing was a formality and not a true testament of his love to the other girl. I began to slowly have hope again that we may still be together. I hung on every word he said. I lived my life waiting on the phone calls he would sporadically make or the letters he would mail. It was the hope that we would one day be together that got me through the last few months of my pregnancy. I decided against giving my baby up for adoption. I just couldn't do it.

On November 10, 1995, I gave birth to my precious son. He was almost nine pounds. I spent almost twenty hours in labor. He was the most beautiful thing I had ever seen in my life. He was so big, so handsome. I would never let him go. Alone in the hospital, I began to cry. I wondered how I would ever provide for this child. What would I do? What was my plan? I looked at how beautiful he was and knew he deserved way more than I could ever give him. The tears flowed most of the night and through the next morning.

I cried for most of the year that followed. I went through the motions of life, caring for my son, but I was not really living. I was merely functioning.

Dillon came home from college two weeks after the birth of our son to see him for the first time. I just knew that once he saw him he would want to quit college, come home, and be the dad that our son so desperately deserved. I know this will shock you, but that never happened. Sure, he held him and commented on how handsome he was. But that was the most he ever offered to our son, a few visits and kind words. After the first time Dillon saw our son, I knew that I had to make plans for our future. Dillon was never going to be there for us. In fact, I had heard that Dillon's second child had been born only a few weeks after my own. My heart ached in a way that I can barely describe, even now. But I had a son to raise and so I pressed on.

Within two weeks, I got my first job. I worked as a waitress for a pizza place. I left my son when he was but ten days old to begin working. I did not have the luxury to rest and recuperate. I got a government-subsidized apartment. I used food stamps and welfare to make ends meet. I hated to use government assistance, but I had no choice. I moved into my new apartment with no furniture, and people slowly donated one piece at a time.

I was making it. I didn't know how, but I was. I was able to get a television and eventually saved up to get cable! I got a phone. I had enough to buy diapers for my baby. I started college at night at the local community college. I made straight A's for the next two years.

My twin sister eventually married a man from our hometown and moved back near me, so she helped me with babysitting also. She helped me with everything! She gave me money to help get my car fixed, to pay my light bill. I eventually moved my baby boy to an in-home day-care facility with my friend, Rhonda. She had operated a daycare for more than twenty years and was well known in the community. She was truly a godsend. She loved my son with all her heart. She cared for him like her own. Many nights, when I would come to pick him up, she would have already fed him dinner and would then offer me a plate. She did not know that I had no food in my pantry. If she would not have fed me so many nights, I would have gone hungry. I am so grateful for her generosity. She became one of my closest friends.

I continued my relationship with Dillon. We talked on the phone and wrote letters several times a week while he was away at college. He had divorced the other girl by then, although I later found out that he was still pursuing a relationship with her, as well. I was holding onto that relationship in hopes that he would one day change. I needed him to help me. I needed him to love me. For once...if I could just have him to love me, we could make our family whole. I would have my happily ever after. I became pregnant again while he was home on his college break. I secretly hoped that this second child would convince him to be with me.

Depression came over me again. How could I tell any of my family or friends that I had done this again? I thought of abortion. I knew it was wrong, deep down, I knew. Yet,

I was so depressed that I feared I couldn't raise another child. My entire world was spinning. I was embarrassed, ashamed, overwhelmed, exhausted, and so much more.

My son was now one-year-old. I had left the pizza place and secured a job as office manager of a local furniture store. I didn't make much money, but it was a nine-to-five-job in a professional environment. I continued to go to college full-time at night, while I worked forty hours a week during the day. I left my son at daycare at eight o'clock in the morning and didn't see him again until ten o'clock that night. I picked him up, put him in bed, and collapsed, all to start again the next morning.

I hid this new pregnancy of my second child for six months. I was only nineteen years old and was pregnant for the fourth time. How had my life gotten so far off track? I dropped out of college. There was no way I could continue to go to school and raise two children while working full-time. I continued working at the furniture store. I went into labor with my twin sister and my "mother," Becky Chapman, there to give support. I gave birth to a beautiful baby girl. She was breathtaking, I must admit. She had lots of curly black hair and pretty tanned skin with big brown eyes and a round face. Just as with my first-born, she, too, was almost nine pounds.

I gave birth to her on a Friday. I went back to work on Monday morning. I had no choice. It broke my heart to leave my newborn so soon. I had no maternity leave, no sick leave. I had no other way of paying my bills, other than to suck it up and press on. I worked hard. If I didn't work, my kids didn't eat.

Dillon came home from college to see our daughter only a few days after she was born. He held her and commented on how beautiful she was, just as he had with our son. But there was no gift, no diapers, and no assistance of any kind. In fact, he mostly complained about how hard college was and how he did not have that much spending money, when all the other students did. All the years my children were in diapers and using baby formula, Dillon never purchased them one item. Nothing. Nada. Some way I convinced myself that he was the pitiful one, all alone in school out of state, with no money, so in addition to everything else, I sent him care packages and money on a regular basis. Any time I got income tax refunds, I sent him money.

He was back and forth away from college during the next two years. He went to school some nine hours away from home. He would come home a few weeks at a time during the summer, but leave shortly thereafter, anything to stay away from his responsibilities. He called, wrote letters, and visited. He continued to manipulate me for years, convincing me that he loved only me and wanted to pursue marriage with me. One night, very late, I received a phone call. The voice on the other end was crying. She began to say, "You don't know me, but Dillon does. And I'm pregnant." The words rang through the night like a bad dream. I held the phone, unable to speak. I felt myself gasping for air. I could not understand how he could do this to me. I could not see how he would have yet another child after not caring for the ones he currently had. I finished that brief conversation in disbelief.

Dillon graduated college a few months later. When I finally saw him, there was an immediate argument regarding that phone call I had received in the middle of the night. "Get out of my life. Get out my house. Stay away from me and these kids!" I screamed. I began to cry and become hysterical. I could not take another second. I could not hurt any more. I could not take another phone call in the middle of the night from another girl. He wrapped his arms around me and began to profess his love to me once again. He claimed that the rumors were all lies. He claimed that those girls were lying. I wanted so desperately to believe him. I wanted for him to keep his arms wrapped around me for the rest of my life. I wanted him to stay with only me. I wanted him to love me the way I loved him, and mostly, I wanted my kids to have their dad. He spent the night that night. He was gone by morning.

Over and over and over again through the next several years, I would let him stay the night, and he would always leave early the next day so that no one saw his car at my house. He disappeared for days on end. He would have no explanation when he returned as to where he had been. I became used to the routine of not knowing where my boyfriend was. I even got used to the endless phone calls that came all hours of the day and night looking for him, or to have some young girl proclaim her love for him and how he wanted to be with her. I remember countless nights of crying and screaming. There was the low self-esteem, the depression. What was wrong with me? Why didn't he love me? What was I doing wrong?

I became so blinded by this infatuation that it never occurred to me to be angry at him for not helping to support his kids. Why didn't he get a job and sacrifice the ways I had? Why was I giving him money? I would do whatever it took for him to be with me. I would storm into his other girlfriend's houses or fight with them. I made countless phone calls looking for him around town. I loaded my children into the car at midnight and rode around looking for him while they slept "in the back seat". For what? So that I could see that yes, his car was at some other girl's house? It was an insane cycle that I thought I would never get away from.

There were many instances of violence throughout my relationship with Dillon. I learned quickly that there would be consequences if I didn't just keep my mouth shut. That's not to say that there weren't times when I didn't just start the argument anyway, because I definitely did.

I was fifteen years old the first time that Dillon became abusive with me. We were sitting in my bedroom. We were having a conversation about how I was talking at school to a friend of mine, who happened to be a boy. He told me that he didn't like when I talked to other boys. It made him uncomfortable. He ran his hands through my long hair and then grabbed me by the hair tightly. His demeanor instantly changed. He whispered in my ear that he did not like it and that he didn't want me talking to this boy again. Very quietly, I said, "Okay," unsure of what had just happened. I now find it ironic that he was so threatened by my other conversations with boys that he would be violent with me, but he, on the other hand, could talk to, kiss, or sleep with any girl he wanted.

I was only a few months pregnant with our second child when the next incident occurred. I was visiting at his parent's home and came outside to leave. I noticed a car sitting nearby and recognized it as an old girlfriend of his. I began to question him about it and was furious by his nonchalant response, I became angry and hysterical. He kept telling me to calm down and the more he did, the louder I got. Before I knew what was happening, he had grabbed my hair and began banging my head against the rear view mirror of his truck. I was so shaken up that I walked away crying and delusional. A few weeks later, just after the birth of our second child, I found him with another girl and flagged him down on the side of the road. He was so angry that I was confronting him that he grabbed my hair and banged my head against the steering wheel over and over, as I sat in my car, with our children. He then threw my keys out the window into a ditch and drove off. How had I fallen into this trap?

Through the seven-year-relationship, there were many instances similar to the above-mentioned. He pulled my hair, choked me, and shoved me around. He would tear up my house, throwing things about the room, breaking them. He screamed and pushed me, and bloodied my ear, once. He threw me to the ground and restrained me many times. I fought back often and had bruises all over me to show it. I never shared with anyone about his violence because I was embarrassed about it and even more embarrassed that I continued to take it. I could not bear for others to know one more thing that would add to the volatility of this relationship. I tiptoed around arguments with him to avoid a confrontation. When he cheated on me, I pretended not to notice or care. I became more and more scared of him.

Time only produced more of the same. I continued to work extremely hard to make ends meet, which barely happened, while Dillon floated from one thing to the next. Sometimes, he lived with me. He rarely worked and had begun to smoke and drink. He jumped from one girl to another and one job to another. There continued to be episodes of violence, emotional abuse, and drug abuse in our home. Our children also continued to grow as Dillon missed more and more birthday parties and Christmases. He never provided one pair of shoes, one diaper, or one meal for our children in those years.

I realize the insanity of this situation now, but at that time, it seemed that Dillon was all I had. I know I didn't truly have him either, but I convinced myself that I did. After seven years in the same situation, I wondered if it would ever end. When would enough be enough? For some of you reading, you cannot imagine taking that many years of abuse or enduring the dozens of instances of infidelity. But for those of you who have endured this same vicious cycle, you understand how hard it is to break free. I pray that the former group will never know this kind of pain.

In those same years, I resumed a relationship with my dad. He moved back to our hometown, where I was living, with his sixth wife, Mary. Daddy had been a smoker for more than fifty years, and it had finally caught up with him. He was dying of cancer. Cancer has a strange way of humbling one. He became a different person. He was easier to talk to, less angry. I watched my dad form a relationship with my children like none other . He adored my kids. He invited them to visit with him at his home, took them driving on Sunday afternoons, and bought them little trinkets. He had stopped drinking a few years prior and seemed to mellow out in his old age.

He knew I had pursued a relationship with Dillon against his better judgment and it angered him, but we rarely talked about it. In those last years of my dad's life, I watched him rededicate his life to the Lord. He dragged his oxygen tank behind him and walked with a cane, but he went to church. He made efforts to call me regularly, and we visited each other often. It seemed that facing his own mortality had significantly increased the importance of knowing his grandchildren.

All I had wanted for so many years was my daddy's love. I saw my dad become more gentle, kind, and loving as he held my children. The last months erased a lifetime of hurt in my life. I was able to release bitterness and anger that I had carried for so long. Forgiveness followed easily. I sat on his bed one afternoon and held his hand. With fear in my heart and a shaky voice, I asked my dad if he was a Christian, if he knew the Lord as his Savior. He said that he knew without a doubt that he was going to heaven and that he was a Christian. Even though I was not living my life fully for God, I took great comfort in hearing those words.

Within a week of that conversation, my twin sister was knocking at my door in the middle of the night to tell me our dad was dead. Cancer had eaten away at his entire body. I was twenty-three years old. The grief that overcame me was like someone releasing all the oxygen from the room. The grief was literally suffocating. I needed to be held, to be comforted. My twin sister had her husband with her, but I had no one. I felt the weight of the world on my shoulders. Now, both my parents were dead. And I had never been more alone.

I stood at my dad's funeral alone, surrounded by friends, yet still alone. The one person that I needed to be there for me wasn't. My kids needed their dad and I needed him too, but he was never there to console me. As the weeks passed, Dillon never said he was sorry about my dad's death. He barely acknowledged it. He never put his arms around me so that I could just cry.

From that moment on, I knew that this season of my life was changing. I didn't know how or why, but I knew my life would never be the same.

CHAPTER 5

HOW DID I WIND UP HERE?

I t is important for me to talk about my emotional state at this point in my life. I do not think you can effectively understand my decisions until you understand the devastation and hurt I was feeling.

I certainly was slowly dying inside.

My self-esteem disappeared. It was a slow process. I did not see it happen, until it was gone. Growing up, I was told often how pretty I was. I was fearless and self-confident, "as every little girl should be". I would sing and dance for family and friends. I was always up for performing a speech or a song. I felt good about myself. Through my early adolescent years, I felt like I could accomplish anything. Yes, I had suffered great pain in my life. But, overall, I still felt like I held the world in the palm of my hand. I could be anything I wanted. Slowly, the years of sexual abuse and the myriad of abusive step moms tore me down.

When Dillon first entered my life, the one thing that stands out above all else is his endless compliments. If I heard it once, I heard a thousand times how beautiful I was. He told me how pretty my eyes were. He brushed my long, brown hair and told me how he loved it. He complimented my figure. He told me how smart I was and how proud he was of me when I would walk across the stage to accept an award at school. I remember one instance where he had walked up to me in the early part of the tenth grade. I looked down to get some papers from a notebook. When I looked up, he just stared at me and said, "God, you are so beautiful!" It is funny that even now, many years later, I can still remember that exact day and how it made me feel. He was showering me with the affirmation that my dad never had.

As this relationship progressed, I began to seek that validation more and more. It mattered what he thought of me. The very course of my day could be determined by whether or not he complimented me or if I caught him talking to another girl that day. It began to determine my self-worth. As with many relationships, the longer we were together, the fewer compliments I received. However, my need for them did not diminish. Because I wasn't getting any validation at home, Dillon became more and more important to me.

Through the years, he became more critical of me. If I wore a shirt or jeans and he said he did not like the way it looked, then I never wore it again. If he said I needed to cut my hair in a particular style, I did. If he said I needed to keep this kind of toothpaste or that kind of cereal in the house, I did. I remember spending hours on my hands and knees scrubbing the kitchen floor on the eve of his arrival home from college, so it would be perfectly clean for him. This was not because he had asked me to, but because I wanted everything to be perfect, free of error, so that he wouldn't want to leave my apartment and go to someone else's apartment. If I saw him showing interest in another girl, I secretly tried to dress like her or wear my hair in a similar fashion. Anything I could do to make myself or my surroundings more appealing to him, I did. It was a sick cycle.

With the arrival of new girlfriends in his life, this process became an obsession. In the years we were together, Dillon pursued dozens of other relationships. Each time he did, I would vow never to speak to him again. With his great persistence, I always gave in. And thus, the cycle would continue. I questioned in my own mind what might be wrong with me. I must not be pretty enough or thin enough. The house isn't clean enough. Everything that could possibly be wrong, I tried to fix. I dieted to lose weight, and then he would say I was too thin. So, then I would eat to gain weight. All of this was an attempt at pleasing him. As you can probably suspect, it never was enough. It never deterred him from doing anything he wanted to do. And I wound up miserable.

By the time Dillon married another woman, my self-esteem was already so low that I didn't think it could get much worse. I was wrong. I had suffered rejection after rejection in this relationship, and countless others before this one, but this was the ultimate blow. To hear that a man you love has chosen someone else to marry and not even told you is beyond comprehension, especially when you spent years deriving your self-worth from him.

As I mentioned earlier, the news of his marriage was so unexpected that I didn't know how to cope. I was eighteen years old and very pregnant with my son at the time. Upon hearing the news, I curled onto the floor in a ball and screamed uncontrollably. I wailed and cried for hours until there were no more tears to shed. My reaction was so severe that my friends discussed hospitalizing me for fear I would lose the baby. I wandered around for weeks afterwards, hopeless.

Within a few months, I had given birth to my son and post-postpartum depression set in. I suffered with depression for over a year. I had lost everything—my family, friends, boyfriend, and my future. I spent my children's toddler years barely functioning. My happiness solely depended on whether Dillon was around. As time passed, he would be in and out of the picture, away at school, then at home again, living with me, and then living with someone else. If he was around and treating me well, then life was grand. Otherwise, I was going through the motions of life.

To add to this depression, my financial situation was dire. Making ends meet was a stretch. I had to calculate down to the penny the gas for my car, rent, and food. There were no extra trips to the grocery store, because I didn't have the gas or the food money to do it. There was no extra money for clothes, so I depended on donations or store credit. For Christmas, we had toys donated to us, and I wrapped them and re-gifted them to the children. I can count on one hand the number of times my children got new clothes in the first several years of their lives. I received a Christmas bonus of $50 on Christmas Eve and I rushed out to buy the kids a new toy each, and pay for our Christmas meal. The kids and I ate alone many Christmases and Thanksgivings, as we patiently waited for Dillon to come around, usually late that evening, after he had visited his own family and his other children.

The shame I carried was almost unbearable. I was embarrassed about my finances. I was embarrassed that my boyfriend had children from one state to another. I carried shame about my past sexual abuse and guilt about my own sexual immorality. I couldn't go back to church because I did not feel good enough to be there. I couldn't tell my friends and family the details of my situation because I knew they would wonder why I had endured the abuses for so long. It all seemed hopeless.

In addition to the financial and relationship struggles, I was hit in the face with blatant racism. As I said earlier, I had never seen a biracial child when I gave birth to my son. That is how uncommon interracial dating in my area was at that time. It was not just that long-term friends avoided or ignored me. It was the constant glares from patrons at restaurants or the rude gestures. It was dealing with the lies that were constantly spread about me around town . My son was called a racial slur at four years old by a fellow preschooler. I even had a stranger come up to me in a local shopping mall and say, "Get out of here and take that little black baby with you." It was horrible and it further alienated me from people.

As the shame and embarrassment was mounting in my own life, my dad had struggles of his own. As I watched him slowly die of cancer, it changed me. I had been as strong as I could for as long as I could. I had been caring for my children alone, working countless hours, because I knew no one else would do it. I stayed up late nights washing clothes and changing bed sheets. I was alone at the hospital when my daughter was hospitalized with pneumonia, when the ambulance came as she vomited blood at two years old. I did all the late-night feedings demanded by infant children. I put myself through school. All of those things were tough, but watching my dad die was by far the toughest. For all of his mistakes, he was still my dad.

His death was the pivotal moment in my life when I knew things would never be the same again. When I watched them lower him into the ground, it was like some of me was buried with him, the bad parts. The shame, embarrassment, and the hurt were all being buried. I knew I had to move on to something new.

CHAPTER 6

A NEW DAY

Several things changed in the twelve months surrounding my dad's death. At the constant urging of my twin sister, I finally visited her church. I had lived my life so far from the things of God that I felt sure He would strike me with lightning as soon as I entered the building. I would like to say that I had a life-changing experience the day I returned to church, but I didn't. I did, however, make a choice to attend again, and then, again.

Before long, I was going three times a week, just as I had as a child.

My life did not change instantly, but I began to find more comfort in church than I ever had. I felt the pastor speaking directly to me in the services and it moved me. It was changing me. I dedicated my free time to volunteering. Any time the church doors opened, I was there.

Just as I had finally found that I was comfortable in a local church, the pastor had nerve enough to preach on tithing! What?! Giving ten percent of my income to the church was not a new concept for me. I had heard this biblical principle while growing up and attending church. The problem was that I had no extra money. How dare he preach on such a thing! As the months went by, I could not get this idea of tithing off my mind. I finally decided to just do it no matter how much money I had. I started giving ten percent of my income faithfully every Sunday.

I had been working at the same furniture store for five years. The company was unable to provide me with benefits or much of a pay raise. There was little opportunity for growth, so I began to search for a new job. I had been happy at the furniture store, and it was definitely my comfort zone by now, but if I was ever going to get off food stamps and welfare, I had to look for something else. I found a job making twice as much money and put in my two weeks notice. The job fell through unexpectedly, and I was left with no job. Within days, a new job "fell" into my lap.

I had no idea what a blessing I had walked into. When I accepted the job, I thought I would be making $22,000 per year. This was far more than the $9,000 per year I had been making, but still barely enough to stay off food stamps. I was still happy with the increased income and newfound benefits, such as medical and dental insurance, childcare, and a 401k retirement plan. I learned my new business quickly. Little did I know, the position I accepted not only had a higher salary, but also provided earning potential from commissions. It is not by accident that I landed this job six months after I began tithing. The day I began tithing, a bill never went unpaid in my home. The money just seemed to always be there.

With hard work and many long hours, I proved to be very good, and sales and commission came easy. I went from making $9,000 a year to six figures annually. The new job afforded me travel opportunities for training and prizes or vacation packages for successful sales months. I went from never leaving my small hometown to travel-ing extensively, dining in fine restaurants, and becoming debt-free. It seemed the more I gave to the Lord, the more financial freedom I experienced.

Although I was beginning to be financially free, I con-tinued to struggle in other areas of my life. I was continu-ing the relationship with Dillon and wrestled with perma-nently leaving him. I continued to sleep with him, but as I became more active in the church, I was more convicted. By the time of my dad's death, I was in an all-out internal war. As much as I loved Dillon, I knew he would never change and I needed a new start. I decided to leave Dillon for good, and I moved to a new town a couple of hours away from him.

As I moved into this new season of my life, I knew there would be hard times. I knew things would be dif-ferent. I would be lying to tell you that I never saw Dillon again. I did invite him to my new home several times, but each time, I knew God was changing me. I did continue to have sex with him sporadically. And each time I did, I felt enormous shame and conviction. I knew I wanted to be closer to God, and Dillon created a barrier. I believe now that God filled me with a new desire in my heart. I believe he filled me with a strength that I had not had before. My heart became hardened towards Dillon, and over that next twelve months, I began to see myself without him. And for the first time, I knew I could make it alone.

There was still an almost unbearable loneliness within me. I wanted to have someone. My kids and I had spent too many holidays alone. I prayed for years that God would somehow make Dillon the one for me, that God would change his heart and turn his life around. I prayed God would show him the error of his ways and make him love me. I was in church on a Sunday morning and was praying that same prayer, even though Dillon and I were no longer together. I secretly still wanted that big, happy family. I began to feel something very vividly in my heart. I can remember that feeling like it was yesterday. It was God telling me not to pray for changes for Dillon, but pray for changes for me. *Begin to pray that you will change, Jennifer.* I believe that day that I did change. I stopped praying for God to send me a godly husband. I began to accept that I was not going to be married, and I was okay with that.

In fact, I was more than okay with the idea of not being married. I began to embrace my singleness. I was overcome with a sense of peace that everything was going to be okay. I had been at the lowest of lows in my life. I had a new attitude. I felt different. I began to feel like I did not need a man to love me. I could make it on my own. I began to feel freedom that my past was my past and God had set forth a new day for me. I was totally at peace with God being the father of my children (in the sense that he was our provider), and I lost the obsession to make their earthly father behave differently.

As I mentioned earlier, I had moved to a new town a couple hours away. I transferred with my company. I walked into the office the first day and was introduced to the staff. One gentleman caught my eye, for no other reason than he was handsome. As the months passed, I began to spend more time with my co-workers. I loved my job so much. The Lord was blessing me immensely, and I was making more money than I had dreamed I could. I continued to tithe and even began giving to missions outreaches and to help other single moms. I no longer had financial struggles. I no longer felt burdened by my past mistakes. I slowly began to think of this new co-worker Jeff as more than a friend.

Jeff was a nice guy. He was a Christian that was active in his local church. He had pretty green eyes with salt and pepper hair. He was just about my age. He had broad shoulders and a nice smile. He was a hard worker, who had become very successful with our company. Perhaps what made him most attractive was his sense of humor and his quick wit that kept me laughing throughout our work days. He did not have any children of his own. When I allowed my mind to stray for a moment, I immediately convinced myself that Jeff would never be interested in me. How could he be? I had so much abuse in my past. I had two children outside of marriage. I was not a good enough Christian. Why would someone who loved the Lord, had a great job, and had no kids want to be burdened with my baggage? Jeff and I went out with groups of friends on occasion. As time passed, I finally got the courage to tell him my true feelings.

Jeff felt the same way, and we began dating. We talked on the phone until the early hours of the morning. We began to take the kids out to dinner. I invited him over for dinner and a movie at my house regularly. It was so exciting. We soon began attending church together. He was great with the kids. I was promoted with our company a few months later and moved away. We continued dating long-distance. Some time later, he transferred with the company to be near the kids and me. He later asked me to marry him. I couldn't believe it. We had won a trip to San Antonio with our company and took a gondola ride on the river through the middle of the city. That evening, we stood on a balcony overlooking the city, and Jeff told me he wanted to spend the rest of his life with me. I was elated. I called everyone I knew and immediately went into planning mode.

We married in early spring of the following year. The wedding weekend was full of the usual hustle and bustle that such an event brings. There were bridesmaids and guests I had not seen in ages arriving from out of town. I was full of emotions, as my bridesmaids and I stayed up most of the night talking and giggling on the eve of my wedding. Then, the day arrived.

I awoke early and rushed around town with last-minute preparations. The bridal party and I had manicures and pedicures. We all had our hair and makeup professionally done. Friends and family helped to get my children dressed as I began the task of climbing into a forty-pound wedding gown. It was a beautiful halter-style floor-length gown with a sweetheart neckline, pearl and sequined beading along the bodice, and a five-foot train. I wore a diamond tiara with a lace wedding veil.

It was an outdoor event of the grandest kind. Jeff and I worked hard in the prior months to pay for every penny, and we did. It was far more than I could have imagined. We were married in a Victorian mansion in the middle of New Orleans, in front of family and friends. The wedding march began to play. I watched as long-time friends marched down the aisle, and I was beaming. But when my children, my little girl in her flower girl dress and my little boy in his tuxedo, held hands and began the journey toward the front of the altar, I lost it. I stood there with tears streaming down my face and a floodgate of emotions overwhelmed me. All the hurt, pain, and disappointments of the past had now been replaced with joy and thanksgiving in my heart. God had truly given me beauty for ashes. I didn't deserve it, but there I stood - fully redeemed, whole, and happy.

We finished the ceremony and danced the night away. All too soon our Rolls Royce limo pulled up to take us to our honeymoon destination. I kissed the kids and hugged friends goodbye. And as we drove away, I knew I was embarking on a new journey, a new life with a wonderful husband. The Lord had finally given me the desires of my heart.

We bought a new home and settled in New Orleans for some years. The home was twice the size of anything I had ever lived in. We stayed faithful to church. Our careers flourished. The children were happy and thriving. We cooked dinner, had family game nights, and vacationed with the children. My heart was full and I was finally free.

I felt free from my past mistakes, my poor choices, the hurt of abuse. All of it was now gone.

A few years later, Jeff adopted my two children. He is now their legal father. He loves them just as if they were his own. And what's more...they love him, too. They are happy and healthy and have grown into a beautiful young man and woman. Today, those kiddos are almost grown. My son has left home and is finishing his college studies and my oldest daughter isn't far behind.

In January 2007, we welcomed home our latest bundle of joy, a beautiful baby girl. Our family is now complete. As I look back over the years of heartache and loneliness, I know that it was merely a season, a short period of time. Oddly, I am thankful for all the challenges and struggles. I grew during that time, and it has allowed me to help others. It was a learning period in my life.

Am I saying that there have not been hard times since I have married Jeff or since I have found Christ in my life? No. I could write another book on the struggles that we have gone through. There have been parenting woes and financial challenges, health and relationship struggles. But God has seen us through it all. However, I have a new hope that surpasses all understanding. I know that no matter what this life brings I am ready. I am armed and prepared. I have a husband that thinks I hung the moon. My heart is full of joy.

God used every piece of my story, every hurt, every tear, to weave together a beautiful ministry. The Life of a Single Mom Ministries was birthed in 2011 to see that no single mom walks alone. I started the ministry as a local service to provide for single mothers any way that we could, but it quickly grew to global status, as we provided a way for churches to best minister to these precious mommas. There is no way I would have had the confidence and strength to launch such a ministry if I hadn't endured those hard, lonely years, and learned to fully trust God. There is no way I could sit with a single mom to counsel her, had I not gone through it also. I praise God for the hard days. It has allowed me to appreciate the easy ones much more!

PART TWO

VICTORY IS WON!

CHAPTER 7

OVERCOMING ABUSE

Abuse comes in all forms; sexual, physical, emotional, and verbal. Every form of abuse is detrimental to your overall well-being. I want to say that again. Every form of abuse hurts. Oftentimes, we make light of emotional and verbal abuse, as if those were less important or less impactful than the others. The truth is, many people can move past the physical beatings much more quickly than they can the words that accompanied them. Have you ever seen a forty-year-old woman say that she can still remember her father telling her that she wasn't pretty? We tend to hang on to verbal abuse for years. The Bible says in James 3:6 that, "...the tongue is a flame of fire. It is a whole world of wickedness, corrupting your entire body. It can set your whole world on fire..." How true.

The home we grow up in is our litmus test on normal. If we heard daily that we were obese, ignorant, or unintelligent, then that is what come to believe. If profanity is used in the household regularly, we soon begin to use it without thinking of it as rude or inappropriate. We become conditioned to accept our environment and usually duplicate it later in life.

Growing up, I was never encouraged to talk about my feelings. If I was hurt or angry or sad and began to cry, I was just sent to my room until I could straighten up my attitude. If I wanted to discuss anything that made my dad uncomfortable, then the subject was changed or there was simply no response. This is true for many homes. Parents do not encourage their children to discuss their emotions, usually because they had their own emotions stifled as a child, or perhaps do not know exactly how to respond, so they avoid it. Either way, the consequences are dire.

Even if everything else was fairly normal in the home, the lack of emotional support and verbal affirmation will soon rear its head as a young woman begins to date. We will discuss parenting in Chapter Ten, but this is why it is crucial that we are equipping our children for emotional well-being.

As young women begin dating, they begin to look for what they are comfortable with. If they are used to their dad screaming at them or their mom using profanity constantly, then it will not seem out of the ordinary when they find it in a boyfriend. Our high schools are plagued with abusive relationships. Many young women do not even know they are in such a relationship until it has escalated to the point of fear that they cannot escape. It may start with an occasional comment, such as, "You sure acted stupid today at school," or "I hate when you wear your hair that way. It makes you look silly." Months or years of hearing these types of comments degrade a young woman, and she begins to lose her self-worth.

Emotional abuse can accompany the verbal abuse or be a different issue altogether. Because adolescent girls are naturally more emotional during the transitional years of puberty, it is expected that there will be what they deem dramatic events in their youth. Boyfriend break-ups are common for the age. However, emotional abuse creeps in when Little Johnny breaks up with her over and over again as an emotional tactic to increase her dependency on him. "I like you today, but I don't like you tomorrow." If a young girl has given herself sexually in this relationship, then the situation escalates. Because teenagers are not prepared for a sexual relationship, young girls can emotionally fall apart when the relationship does not work out. Infidelity can creep into the relationship. The boyfriend will use her and dump her, and then eventually wants her back again. This scenario repeats itself in our high schools and colleges across the country. Our young women are so distraught from suffering with emotional and verbal abuse that by the time they reach adulthood, they do not know how to function in a normal, healthy relationship. Their whole view on relationships is tainted.

This does not stop with adolescence. It is amazing

the number of women I counsel that have endured years of abuse as a child or teenager and then find themselves in an abusive adult relationship, as was the case with me. She wakes up to a man that she married who has devalued her for years, or dated the same boyfriend for years, and he does the same thing. What's worse is seeing her jump from one abusive relationship to another because she doesn't feel she deserves more.

It is the same for physical and sexual abuse. Many people make comments such as, "Why won't she just leave him? Why does she continue to take it over and over again? Can't she figure out that he is going to do this to her again?" These are clearly the comments of someone who has never experienced abuse or has not been properly educated about its affects. If a woman entered a relationship with little self-esteem (perhaps stemming from her childhood, or if her esteem has been drained through her current relationship, then she does not believe she can do better or even deserves better. If her very existence and self-worth was derived from her relationship with a man, then when he becomes abusive, she convinces herself that she cannot leave him because she needs him.

As with the other forms of abuse, physical abuse starts slowly. For me, I had my hair pulled at fifteen years old. It was not enough to hurt me, but it scared me. I later thought that he only did it because he loved me and was hurt that I had talked to another boy. He wouldn't do that again. I was sure that I had overreacted. That made the second and third offenses easier to get through. Before I knew it, being pushed or shoved or having my hair pulled was just part of a typical Saturday night.

It breaks my heart each time I work with a young

girl and her story of abuse unfolds. She tells me how he didn't mean to do it and he will not do it again. She makes excuses by explaining what she did that made him so angry. It is never long before I see the same girl come back with bruises on her arms or a black eye and I immediately know. I just know.

As abuse victims, we get so wrapped up in the emotions of the relationship that we cannot see straight. We need our spouse/boyfriend to love us. We need him to give us value. We do not understand why he is doing what he is doing, but maybe if we just talk less or if we try not to upset him, then he will stop. "If I wasn't so annoying, then maybe he would not do this anymore," we tell ourselves. The attachment becomes so great that the longer we are in the relationship, the harder it is to visualize ourselves without him.

Sexual abuse is such a delicate subject. Because of the immense shame surrounding such abuse, many women never confess these victimizations. The most recent statistics supports at least 25% of all women have been sexually abused. Those are the ones who have reported it. Rape and molestation are the most common forms of abuse. Inappropriate touching and/or unsolicited sexual conversations, such as with a minor, are also considered abuse. Exposure to pornography is also a common form of sexual abuse. Many instances of childhood sexual abuse is usually not violent, therefore children are not sure what just happened. All they know is that they do not feel right about the episode, but they are sometimes not sure whether or not to tell someone. In adult relationships, some women have even been raped by their boyfriend or husband and do not consider it abuse. They simply feel that if they are in a relationship with him, then his sexual advances are required, even if she refuses them.

It is hard to pinpoint which form of abuse damaged me the most, but I can tell you that viewing pornography as a child ranks highly on the list. For years, I had no idea that it was considered abuse. The only word I can use to describe how I felt as a ten-year-old child being forced to watch such filth is icky. It made me feel icky. In viewing it, I cannot tell you that I understood much of what I saw, but there was a sick feeling in the pit of my stomach. I covered my eyes and looked away. I was instantly ashamed, even though it was not by my choosing. Something deep within me told me that it wasn't right. Now, many years later, I am haunted by the things I saw back then. It is a constant source of prayer that I will keep my thoughts pure and if my mind travels back there, I immediately refocus.

Through the years, I became desensitized to seeing graphic images. I watched movies with illicit sex. I listened to music with sexually explicit lyrics. I had no qualms with seeing anything of a sexual or violent content. It all stemmed from having watched pornography as a child, as well as total disregard by my parents for what I viewed. It scarred me. I carried the shame around for years. Through counseling women, I have heard more stories of sexual abuse than I can remember or even care to. Each time a woman opens up and shares this horror, I am overwhelmed with compassion. My heart breaks for I know that it is a long journey through recovery. And it doesn't matter how much her family or friends think she should do it. Only she can choose to embark upon such a journey.

I was once invited to speak at a ladies' meeting where I shared my personal story. I had finished speaking and the event was coming to a close. There was a woman in her mid-forties sitting in a chair across the room, crying softly. After the room cleared, I walked over to her and gently put my arm around her. She began to slowly share her story with me. I sat and cried with her as she released this heavy burden of sexual abuse. We held hands and prayed. Her story was so horrid that as I later drove from the parking lot, I had to pull over. I was physically ill at the thought of what so many women have to endure.

At another women's fellowship, I was sitting in the back of the room as a young girl in her early twenties shared her story with me of having been raped as a teenager. As she brought her story to completion, she asked if anyone had any questions or comments they would like to share. A woman, perhaps in her fifties, raised her hand and began to share. None of us expected what we heard next. Tears streamed down her face as she spoke. She told the story of how she had dated the same man for over ten years and shared a child of with him. He had beaten her regularly. She was trying to leave him and had taken her daughter one night. As they began to walk a few blocks away to a relative's home, he followed her. He was furious that she was leaving him and he began to beat her in the street. She sent her daughter to run to the relative's home. The woman began to run, as her boyfriend hit her repeatedly in the face. He tackled her to the ground and she pulled a gun from her purse. He wrestled the gun from her and beat her across the face. He raped her in the middle of someone's driveway at only ten o'clock at night. As she told her story over the next fifteen minutes, you could have heard a pin drop.

After she finished, no one said a word. We sat in

silence for several minutes. The speaker then asked if there were others in the room that had been raped or molested. Several nodded, and as we began to look around the room, more than seventy-five percent of that room had suffered such atrocities.

In this book, I chose to only mention a couple incidents of sexual abuse in my past. I did not go into details, give names, or recite every incident. I did this for a few reasons. One of the biggest reasons is that I have totally forgiven all the individuals that participated in those events. I harbor no anger or bitterness. I am living in total freedom over my past. The other reason I don't share every incident is because you likely couldn't bear to hear it all. It would turn your stomach, haunt your imagination, and keep you awake at night. There were many more instances of sexual abuse that I could have talked about with more perpetrators. In fact, I could have written pages on the events. But I simply wanted you to know that I am a victim as well, and I got through it. That's the most important message you need to hear. I got through it and am healthy. You can, too.

For some of you who read my story, you could relate on many levels. Others of you have read in awe of why one person would take so much abuse. You wondered at some point, "When is enough, enough? When is she going to move on with her life and leave this guy alone? What is wrong with her?" Have you ever heard the saying, "You cannot see the forest for the trees"? I guess that is the best way to describe an abusive relationship.

Each time an incident would take place in my own relationship, I would vow that was it. I would be determined to end the relationship. And every time I did, he would come on stronger. It's like that, sometimes. As you try to end a relationship of any kind with a party that is not adding value to your life, they oftentimes will come back with a vengeance, wanting to convince you they are worthy of your time. For an abused woman, this can be the cycle that will not end. Because you have been through past abuse, your self-esteem is low. Your self-confidence is down. You cannot imagine yourself deserving better. Who would want you, anyway? Because you have those feelings, you begin to allow events to take place in your relationships that an otherwise healthy woman would not. You tolerate abuse. You settle for it.

As I look back through my past, one thing is for certain. I needed to be loved. Every time a new stepmom entered my life, I called her "momma" and embraced her with open arms. Later, I accepted every apology my boyfriend gave to me over his indiscretions. I needed someone to think I had value. I needed someone to love me. I needed to be validated, to feel I was worthy of such love.

According to an article published *by Aphrodite Women's Health* on March 14, 2007, fifty percent of all sexually abused children come from a single parent home. Thus, my passion for the betterment of single mothers overtakes me. How can I not address how to recover from this hurt? As single mothers who are victims of abuse, you can sometimes be so blinded by your own past abuse that you are not fervently looking to protect your own child. As sad as that sounds, we can fall into that trap very quickly. Many times, single moms are in such depression and loneliness that they invite a man into their home to fill that void in their lives, not thinking of the potential dire consequences. It only takes a minute for your son or daughter's life to be altered forever, so we must be fervent in our own recovery, so that we are healthy enough to properly raise our children.

In my own personal experience, as well as through the many women I have worked with, I have found a common thread. As abuse victims, it is easy to allow those events to shape the rest of your life. If you do not spend time healing, you will become obsessed with the event. You will think on it day and night. Your every decision will revolve around the abuse. You cannot effectively parent. You cannot function. It holds you hostage. Every relationship going forward is ruined or tainted. You manipulate your future relationships so that you will not have to deal with the hurt and pain inside.

Can I tell you that it will never end if you do not take control of it? When I think of my own journey through the healing process, I think of it as a step-by-step recovery. I did not magically transform into a healthy person. I did not even know that I was mentally unhealthy for many years. I was in my mid-twenties before I ever had the nerve to talk about all that happened to me.

I strongly recommend counseling. In fact, I do not believe you can survive or truly thrive unless you do seek help. As a single mom, I know that money can be an issue in paying for such services. Begin to pursue your local church. Oftentimes, they have licensed or trained counselors on staff that can begin to work with you through your pain. If your personal church does not offer such support, then you can search for other area churches. Many local communities have free or nearly-free community counseling centers. Start somewhere. Do not put it off. Do not say that you do not have time. You do not have time *not* to get counseling. For every day that you put it off, you are losing precious time with your own children; time when you could be healthy and embracing life fully.

You need to be able to release what you are carrying around. Once you talk about it, you will begin to slowly feel a burden lifted from your shoulders. You will breathe easier. This is not an overnight process. I do not want to give the impression that it is. I do not pretend to be an expert at the ins and outs of the human psyche. I can only speak to what I know is true in my own life and those that I have counseled. The more I have talked about my abuse, the more freedom I have experienced. It no longer holds me hostage. It is no longer "everything" in my life but merely something.

From the first time I uttered the words, I was free. The years of embarrassment began to slowly dissipate. For every time I shared my story, it could no longer suffocate me or hold me in bondage. I was no longer a slave to the thoughts that had held me captive. The weight of the world was off me. The same can be true for you.

One of the most difficult things to live through, for me, was the shame. Logically, I know that the abuse was not my fault. I could not have prevented it. I could have done nothing differently. But in the midst of my pain, I could not see that. I lived with the shame that somehow I was wrong. I was dirty. I lived with the feeling of being used goods, no longer wanted by anyone. What's worse is that I could not talk about it. I felt that no one would believe me. I thought I would be laughed at or made fun of. No one would care. I felt this was something that I should just "get over." So, I swept it under the rug for many years. Only now do I have the freedom that I once longed for. I carried this desire to share it, but lived in shame to say the words aloud. I no longer feel that shame and embarrassment.

In addition to counseling, you must have a strong prayer life. Prayer played an important role in my recovery. There were certain things that I knew no one else would understand or I couldn't bring myself to tell anyone else. I had to learn to lean on God. I spent many nights on my knees crying out to God with my pain. I asked repeatedly for help in forgiving those who had hurt me. I asked him to heal my pain, my embarrassment, and my shame. And little by little, he did.

I grabbed every book I could find on sexual healing from a Christian perspective. I loved how I could read and then re-read a section or chapter until I got it. It was awesome to see how a particular chapter in a book would not mean anything to me at first, but as I grew in my recovery, it resonated loud and clear.

And lastly, you need a mentor, someone who has gone through abuse and is now recovered. This person will help keep you accountable to following your recovery plan issued by your counselor. She will also lend a shoulder to cry on during those crucial, but difficult facets of your recovery. We all need to lock arms with someone who is stronger than us that can help encourage us and lift us up. It's important that you know that your boyfriend (if you have one) cannot replace a mentor. He is not far enough removed from the situation. Be sure to pray about who God would have for you that can help you in your journey ahead.

There is no one thing that will allow your feelings or hurt to disappear. You must actively pursue your own recovery. Get the counseling you need. Pray. Read books. And get a mentor. Decide that it will take some time, but make the decision now. I know in the middle of your hurting that few words make a difference. I pray that as you read this chapter again and again that its words will begin to minister to your very soul, that somehow you can release some of the past pain. I know that as you find a counselor, mentor, and spiritual leader, such as a minister or pastor, to begin to confide in about these tragedies in your life, you will feel the same freedom I now have.

Scripture says in John 8:36, "Whom the Son sets free is free indeed." I invite you to stand on that word. God is telling you that there is freedom in Christ. He is saying that all the sins in the world and all the bondages that we often find ourselves in will not stand, if we truly get set free through Christ.

I do not know your exact story. I am not walking through your pain. But I am giving you hope that there is freedom from it all. I am encouraging you that you can get through it. I want to inspire you to search for that recovery, to reach for it. I want to give you hope that there is freedom in Christ. There is a place that you can get to where there is no more bitterness or un-forgiveness in your soul.

Do not give up or give in. Assuredly, the road to recovery will get hard. But you cannot live your life in a bubble of defeat, heartache, and shame. Do it for your children. Do it for you.

OVERCOMING ABUSE
WEEK 1

Have you suffered with abuse, in any form, as a child or adult? Do you know someone who has? What are your thoughts and feelings about the abuse?

_____

_____

_____

_____

Oftentimes, women do not feel that verbal abuse is as harmful to them as physical or sexual abuse. Read James 3:6 and write it here. What does this tell us about our words?

_____

_____

_____

_____

Think about a time in your life when you were rejected. How did you handle it?

_____

_____

_____

_____

For many women, they carry abuse and rejection from their past for many years. Commit today to a plan of releasing this past hurt. Write your plan here.

_____

_____

_____

_____

_____

_____

_____

PRAYER:

Lord, I have suffered so much pain from the past that I cannot carry it anymore. I give it to you, today. Give me wisdom today as I begin to release hurt, pain, and bitterness. Direct my path on the next steps that you would have me to take for ultimate healing. Amen.

OVERCOMING ABUSE
WEEK 2

As we continue to discuss abuse, it is likely that you will deal with several emotions through this process. I recommend counseling. Write the names and phone numbers of local churches or community organizations that provide free counseling in your area.

_____

_____

_____

_____

It is crucial that we have friends to share our stories with. Was there a difficult time in your past that a friend helped you through? Describe it here.

_____

_____

_____

_____

Write the names of two or three close friends that you feel comfortable confiding in.

_____

_____

_____

_____

Is there anything that you are carrying from your past that you have not told anyone? How do you think you would feel if you shared it?

_____

_____

_____

_____

What is the number one thing you would like your children to know about abuse? What measures have you put in place to avoid abuse in your own home?

_____

_____

_____

_____

PRAYER:

Father, allow me to begin today anew. Allow me to make a new start. Give me fresh perspective. I ask for total freedom. I pray that I will continue to work on my own healing, so that I can be healthy for my children. Give me strength to endure my recovery. Amen.

CHAPTER 8

BEING A SINGLE PARENT

Change can be difficult. There is a transition that takes place when you become a parent, married or not. This change becomes far greater if you are moving into the single parent world and doing it all on your own. This book is written to encourage all single mothers: divorced, unwed, and widowed. The more I thought about each of these separate groups, the more I realized that no matter how you arrived at single parenthood this journey is going to be similar.

With the exception of widows, single parenting didn't happen instantly. It was a process. Whether you had an unexpected pregnancy or went through a treacherous divorce, we can all agree that it did not happen in the blink of an eye. If you had a drunken one-night stand or have had a long history of sex outside marriage, it is safe to say that having a baby was not the plan. Or maybe you married Mr. Right and it turned out to be wrong. Regardless of whose fault the failed marriage was, we can again assume that you had not planned to parent alone. It usually takes many months and sometimes many years for a marriage to end in divorce. Consequently, becoming comfortable in the role of a single mom will take time.

Patience is the key. And if you are anything like me, this is a tough one. I am an instantaneous girl. I want whatever problem I am dealing with to be fixed and over before the sun goes down. That wouldn't require much patience, would it? You must give yourself time to go through the myriad of emotions you are undoubtedly experiencing. Allow yourself time to regroup and decide what path you are now on.

There are four common areas that I have found most single moms struggling with:

- financial burden

- emotional stress

- parenting concerns, and

- the pursuit of spiritual growth.

I dedicated an entire chapter to both parenting and finances, so I will address emotional stress and spiritual growth here.

I told you earlier about how I grew up in and out of

church. I then discussed how I returned to church and developed a strong relationship with God. I cannot go further without telling you step by step how to become a Christian. For I believe whole-heartedly that I can give you all the parenting or financial advice known to man, but if you have not accepted Christ as your Savior, then you will still be unable to find true happiness.

Galatians 5:22–23 says, "But the Holy Spirit produces this kind of fruit in our lives: love, joy, peace, patience, kindness, goodness, faithfulness, gentleness, and self-control."

Love? "Love makes the world go 'round," they say. In the middle of parenting a child alone and trying to stretch a dollar to put food on the table, can you even fathom love, peace, and joy? Most of you cannot. You want that peace, but it seems your whole world is flipped upside down. You may be trying to work three jobs to make ends meet. You may be rushing little Johnny from ball practice to band practice. You don't know which way to turn. You are tired. What about kindness and gentleness? Has there been a time when you were parenting that you wished you had been a little more kind and gentle with your toddler or teenager? Do you wonder what is wrong with you? "Am I the only parent on earth that screams profanities at my kids?" you may wonder. These are the things that God's Word says he will provide: peace, joy, and love.

Do you know that if I depended on my husband as my source, even now, I would be disappointed? I have talked about what an awesome husband I have. I have mentioned how he loves the Lord and puts him above all else. I talked of how he treats me like a queen. I also mentioned that none of us could be a perfect man or woman, but we can be the perfect one for our spouse. That's all true. No matter how hard my husband tries, there will be times when he makes mistakes, as will I. If I lean on him to be the source of my happiness and joy, then I lose. I come up empty. Does he bring joy into my life? Of course, he does. My children do. My friends and family also do. But none of those people are the source of my joy, peace, and happiness. They don't complete me. Those things are rooted in my faith and only my heavenly Father can provide those things.

For some of you, you have gone through your whole life looking for the void in your heart to be filled. You have felt a hole. You have sought relationships that failed. You have been abandoned by family and friends. The church has failed you. You do not know where else to turn. The hole in your heart can only be filled with Jesus Christ. Let me be real with you. There is nothing wrong with you desiring to be married, be loved, and have the white picket fence with two beautiful children. God made us for relationships. However, when we look to another human being to be our source of joy and hope, we will always be disappointed. There is no man or woman on earth that can be perfect; no perfect friends, no perfect parents. We all strive to be those things, but only God is perfect.

In the midst of my drama, I always desired to be loved. Somehow, I thought having sex at thirteen years old would make me feel complete. It would make me feel loved. I thought partying all night at the local club scenes could mask my insecurities. I convinced myself it was fun. And maybe it was for a few brief moments. I moved from one relationship to another, finally settling into a seven-year relationship that I should have moved on from years earlier. None of it helped. I was constantly empty. I was not looking to Christ as my source.

You have to be whole in Christ. Your whole identity cannot be wrapped up in material things, such as clothes or shoes. And it cannot be wrapped up in multiple sexual partners or dancing all night at the clubs. I have seen women addicted to everything: shopping, pornography, sex, drugs, and alcohol. Some don't even realize the addiction. Usually from years of pain, they grasp at something to help ease their pain. When reaching for these things, they come up short. You must be complete, looking to God as your source of strength, in order to live a full life. Am I saying every day will be perfect with sunshine and roses? Will you never have trouble? I am not saying that. I am saying the Lord gives you hope that you can make it through. And the peace comes from deep within, not just some temporary high that we can get on from alcohol or drugs.

God made us with a desire to be loved and to worship. Some of you (like me) have spent years worshiping men, sex, drugs, alcohol, pornography, or money. Yet, you always wind up feeling empty. You may not have referred to it as worshiping, and you may not have been addicted to it, but that thing, whatever it was, became your source of happiness. You have spent your life wandering from one self-fulfillment to another, and still couldn't understand why you weren't happy. You may have even tried the whole church thing. It is not church, not religion, but rather a relationship with Christ that delivers us true happiness.

I will share with you what I call Christianity 101—Bible basics. It doesn't matter what church you choose or what denomination you pursue. (Do your homework and pray that God will lead you to a good, Bible-based church where you can grow.) But the most important steps are as follows:

1. Recognize what sin is.

James 4:17 says, "It is sin to know what you ought to do and then not do it."

2. Recognize that you are a sinner and what the consequence of sin is.

Romans 3:23 says, "For everyone has sinned and fallen short of God's standard."

Romans 6:23 says, "For the wages of sin is death."

3. Repent. Believe Jesus is the son of God.

John 3:16 says, "For God so loved the world that he gave his one and only Son , so that everyone that believes in him will not perish but have eternal life."

John 14:6 says, "Jesus said, 'I am the Way, the Truth, and the Life. No one can come to the Father except through me'."

Romans 10:9–10 says, "If you confess with your mouth that Jesus is Lord and believe in your heart that God raised him from the dead, you will be saved. For it is by believing that you are made right with God, and it is by confessing with your mouth that you are saved."

You can become a Christian anywhere—in a church service or on your bedroom floor. Once you become a Christian, you will want to learn more through God's Word, prayer, and church attendance.

I have seen women in their twenties that desperately search for something in their lives. They do not know exactly what, but something. Unfortunately, I see that same search for inner peace coming from women in their fifties and sixties. The search is not age specific. I see women jumping to the latest fad religion and losing interest in it after it does not bring the everlasting joy that they hoped it would. Here again, it's all about a relationship, not a religion.

As you are navigating through this season in your life, there is another big piece of the puzzle, emotions. I was thinking about the widowed mother and what devastation she must go through. I have experienced death, but never that of a spouse. When you look into the eyes of your children, I know you are at a loss as to the perfect words to say. But as I thought on that, I realized the same can be true of an unwed or divorced mother. It is not uncommon that grief would strike a mother who just lost a relationship that she thought was going to last. It is natural to mourn the loss of what could have been, what you hoped for.

Grief can move us right into loneliness and depression. Depending on the severity, depression allows our mind to play tricks on us. We start self-doubting. "I'll never find someone like Bobby," you may begin to think. "I'll always be alone. God doesn't have anyone for me. He doesn't care about me." You start thinking about all the things you could have done differently. You beat yourself up with coulda, shoulda, woulda's.

The emotional journey can also bring bitterness, anger, and un-forgiveness. They sneak up on you just the same way as loneliness and depression. You start by thinking about one incident that went wrong, one time that you were treated poorly, and it escalates to epic proportions. You think about every time your husband mistreated you, especially if you were abused. Everything angers you, past, and present. You are furious about your finances and aggravated about your children's disobedience. Be careful. You do not want to become a seventy-year-old, enraged, bitter, grandmother that people avoid like the plague.

> Get rid of all bitterness, rage, anger, harsh words, and slander, as well as all types of evil behavior. Instead, be kind to each other, tenderhearted, forgiving one another, just as God through Christ has forgiven you.
>
> Ephesians 4:31–32

Talk about wise counsel! Let go of all the bitterness, anger, and un-forgiveness. It will eat you alive, if you don't. Many times, we do not forgive because we want to hurt the other person emotionally. It always backfires. The sooner you can let go, the better.

Celebrate small accomplishments. If you had the urge to scream at your child and you didn't, then celebrate it (even if you screamed at him three hours later). Start with baby steps. Loneliness, grief, bitterness, anger, and un-forgiveness will take time to deal with, so be prepared. Reward yourself for all small victories. (If you are suffering from severe, on-going depression, seek medical help.)
Finally, remember this is only a season of your life, a small window of time in your eighty- or ninety-year journey. Children grow up. They move away. You will make it through this time. Don't focus on trying to find a new man

to have a new husband or dad for your children. God will handle that in his timing, if he desires that for your life. But do focus on being the best mother, friend, sister, and Christian you can be. When you do that, you will not lose who you are in this process.

BEING A SINGLE PARENT
WEEK 3

What are the four most common areas that single moms struggle with?

_____

_____

_____

_____

Which one do you feel is the most difficult for you? Why?

_____

_____

_____

_____

Read Galatians 5:22–23. Which of these qualities do you most desire in your life?

_____

_____

_____

_____

Write the most disappointing thing you have experienced during this transition to single parenting. Was it your fault? Whether you answered yes or no, release yourself right now from this disappointment.

_____

_____

_____

_____

Is there something that you have spent years addicted to, e.g. men, sex, drugs, money, alcohol, shopping, or partying? When you think about that activity, does it bring you true joy?

_____

_____

_____

_____

Write the three steps to becoming a Christian here.

_____

_____

PRAYER:

Dear God, I ask forgiveness for my sins. I have failed. It has left me empty. Fill me with joy. I believe you sent your son to die for my sins. I want to change my life and live for you. Please help me. Amen.

CHAPTER 9

PLAYING THE VICTIM ROLE

I recently heard a pastor speak on truth. He talked about how the Bible is full of truth. The Bible says the truth sets us free. He went on to later say that there are times in our lives that it is easy to twist truth to fit our situation or make it comfortable for us, especially when we do not like what the truth really is. We have all heard that old adage that the truth hurts.

That statement will be true of what you are about to read, so be prepared. It must be said.

First, let's talk about hurt. There are dozens of ways that you could have suffered hurt in your life. You could have suffered severe sexual trauma, such as rape or molestation. Maybe you have been beaten or verbally abused. Perhaps you grew up in a home with alcoholism or suffered through another traumatic event, such as death, divorce, or neglect. The list goes on and on. How we handle the hurt is crucial to our future.

There is an appropriate time for dealing with hurt. The Bible talks about going through different seasons of life. It is healthy to mourn the loss of a loved one after a death. It is normal to have anger or hurt after you have been wronged or abused. That is appropriate and expected. Here is when we get into the danger zone, when we cannot move past the hurt. This is especially true for victims of violent crime or abuse.

I am not going to tell you what is an appropriate time to go through a particular emotion. What took me two months to recover from may take you two years. Each person grieves differently. Everyone has a process of recovery to go through. The aftereffects of divorce or abuse can be mind-blowing and take months or years to work through. The important thing is that you do work through it. The event will paralyze your life until you do.

For example, the loss of a child is devastating. I have known many people that have suffered such a loss. But I have also known women that ten years later are still mourning the loss almost daily. Is this to say that you ever stop missing the child or wonder what could have been of their life? Of course not. This was your child, your flesh and blood. They will always hold a special place in your heart.

The same is true for abuse. Let's say you were raised by a drug-addicted mother. She beat you and was sexually promiscuous. She verbally assaulted you on a regular basis. It is okay for you to have hurt and anger. But what quality of life will you have if you do not deal with the hurt from your past?

I want to be extremely clear. I do not dare minimize the pain associated with death, divorce, abuse, and other trauma. Not at all. I have personally walked through most of that tragedy. It is tumultuous. It hurts. You are on an emotional roller coaster that does not seem to end. I have tremendous compassion for those suffering through such events.

But until you deal with the events, you are immobilized. You function through life fairly normal, but no one knows the hurt you carry deep within you. When you do not seek out the necessary tools to help you, the event defines the rest of your life. It is not just a part of your life. It becomes your whole life. You become a victim, not a mom, sister, or daughter, but a victim only.

When we have had a rough childhood or hurt and abuse in our past, possibly from a previous relationship, it is very easy to slip into the victim role. We get so caught up in wanting to be right, wanting to seek revenge on those that hurt us, or wanting someone to feel sorry for what has been done to us that we do not give it to God. We lose focus. The past consumes us. We never move forward to the present.

Some of you cannot stop speaking negativity over your life. *I am too fat. I am not pretty enough. I do not have that great of a personality. I have no friends. My children never obey me. You do not understand how I feel. I was abused.* Stop doing that! When you do that, you begin to believe those things. They become your truth.

Consider the story of Job, as told in the book of the Bible by the same name. Job was considered a wealthy man in his day. He had a flourishing family and business. He was admired by his family and the community. He was considered a God-fearing man and was obedient to follow God's will for his life. He was righteous, a man of complete integrity. He was an all-around good guy. Satan approached the Lord one day about Job. He told the Lord that Job was only faithful because the Lord had prospered him greatly, but if the Lord took away all his wealth, then he would curse God. The Lord agreed to allow Satan to take away all of Job's wealth. He lost his business. Job continues to praise God, even though he has lost all wealth. Satan comes back again and is granted permission to take away Job's family, so they all died. He later takes away Job's health, and he becomes very sick. He still continues to praise God. Job's friends began to falsely accuse him of sin. They tell him that he must have done something to deserve this.

Job lost everything: family, friends, money, and health. Yet, he continued to praise God. He never blamed him. At the end of the story, God restores Job to far more than he had before. He raises up more children for Job. He gives him more wealth than he once had. His health is restored. Have you ever been in that kind of situation? Have you lost all your money? Your reputation? Your family? Use Job as an example in your own life. Job had two choices. He could blame God for his hardship or he could praise God for his goodness. He could deal with his temporary hurt, knowing that God is always faithful to supply all our needs.

In my years of working with women, I have heard almost every story imaginable. I think of the woman who told me she watched her husband burn to death in a fire. I think of the seventy-year-old widow who endured thirty-seven years of physical beatings before her husband died. I think of the young girl who was raped and the rapist later approached her to deliver her undergarments back to her. I think of the breast cancer survivor who lost both breasts. Do you know what is amazing about each and every one of these women? They are all serving the Lord faithfully and have gone on to live happy, healthy lives after the tragedy. They have claimed their victory, and the chains of the event hold them no more.

Sometimes it is easier to complain about our situation than to do anything about it. The bitterness and unforgiveness are like a cancer that is eating you up, but you will not get chemotherapy. I understand. I know the hurt and pain of disappointment after disappointment. I know the pit we can sometimes find ourselves in. Sorrow comes in many packages. We hide it well. We imagine the perfect home with a loving spouse, plenty of money, and obedient children. We imagine the perfect job. When those things don't happen, it is so easy to become absorbed in the pain.

There is a time for mourning. There is a time to grieve for what you have lost, whether it is a death or a failed relationship. It is okay to miss that relationship. But you must realize that your personal joy is not someone else's responsibility. You choose to get up. If we are not careful, depression, loneliness, suicidal thoughts, feelings of inadequacy, self-pity, self-esteem issues, self-consciousness, and the feeling of being overwhelmed can sneak up on us. We look up one day, and we have nothing to live for. We cannot find joy. The joy of the Lord is your strength.

When it gets so bad that you literally do not know how you are going to pay the light bill, there is hope. When you aren't sure where your next meal is coming from, or how you can pay your house note, is sometimes our darkest hour. When we are overcome with pain over past hurt, we have to stand on the promises of God. We have to believe that there is hope. If we give up, then we are done. Our children have a fruitless life. Our children suffer. Don't you want to be the very best parent you can? Of course, you do. We all do. There is encouragement all over the scripture that we can cling to in the middle of our storm. Here are just a few:

> Daniel 6:26–27 ... For he is the living God, and he will endure forever. His kingdom will never be destroyed, and his rule will never end. He rescues and saves his people; he performs miraculous signs and wonders in the heavens and on earth.

> Isaiah 41:9–10 I took you from the ends of the earth, from its farthest corners I called you. I said, You are my servant. I chose you and have not rejected you. So do not fear, for I am with you; do not be dismayed, for I am your God. I will strengthen you and help you; do not be dismayed for I am your God. I will strengthen you and help you; I will uphold you with my mighty right hand.

> Psalm 57:2 I will cry out to God most High, to God who performs all things for me.

Matthew 15:32 Jesus called his disciples to him and said, "I have compassion for these people."

Through the above verses, we can find strength. God is telling us that he has compassion on us, that he loves us, and that he will not reject us. He wants us to lean on his strength. It is yours for the taking. All you have to do is ask him for it.

Proverbs 19:3 says, "People ruin their lives by their own foolishness and then are angry at the Lord." Ouch! I think we can all agree that as we have walked through this life there have been things that we have messed up and also things that were done to us. There were mistakes made. In the midst of these mistakes, we can be quick to blame God. We take our anger out on him. "How could you do this to me? Why me?" We may cry out.

Be careful not to live in blaming God or others for your situation. It does not matter if someone else caused it. When we blame others and carry the bitterness that it brings, we hurt. We do not cause harm to the other person. Along with blaming others, we sometimes blame God. I do not understand everything that happens on this earth. I cannot wrap my mind around why there are starving children or disease or why bad things happen to seemingly good people. I have been asked about those things many times by non-believers.

Here is my response. I turn to God's Word again.

My thoughts are nothing like your thoughts and my ways are far beyond anything you could imagine. For just as the heavens are higher than the earth, so my ways are higher than your ways and my thoughts higher than your thoughts.

Isaiah 55:8–9

God is saying He has all this under control. He tells us clearly that there are things we are not going to under- stand because he is far smarter and deeper than us. The depth of his knowledge is something we cannot even wrap our brains around! There is another scripture I have clung to through the years:

All things work for the good of those who love the Lord and are called according to his purpose.

Romans 8:28

For so long, I could not understand why I was molested. Why did my dad turn his back on me? Why was I the vic- tim of an abusive relationship? Why? Why? Why? Well, I got tired of wondering why those things happened! It does not matter. It really doesn't. There is not one thing that can be done about your past. There is not one thing you can say that will change what has happened to you. The only thing that is different is how you handle your future. I made a decision to not let anything from my past control my future. I decided to not be bitter at God, but to accept that there were things that I didn't understand. Romans 8:28 is probably one of my favorite scriptures of all time. I quote it often. The Bible does not say that if you are a Christian that everything good will happen to you. It says that even the bad things will work out for your good in the end.

How has that happened for me? There is not one event in my life that has not shaped me to be stronger and more sensitive. The events have allowed me to reach out to other hurting women and help them. A long time ago I was faced with a decision of whether or not to continue to live in the misery that was my life. I chose to change it. I praise God for the strength that I needed to do that. I prayed daily for that strength and it did not happen instantly, but when it did, I seized it.

What is the alternative? Stop and think about it for a minute. If you do not seize God's word and begin the journey to recovery, what happens? You continue to question God. You continue to live in offense, looking for someone to hurt like you have been hurt. You look for someone to blame. The end result is complete misery. You remain the victim. Praise God that he has promised us victory. Yours is there for the taking.

PLAYING THE VICTIM ROLE
WEEK 4

What has been the biggest source of hurt and pain from your past? How long ago did it happen?

_____

_____

_____

_____

Have you dealt with the pain? Why or why not?

_____

_____

_____

_____

Do you believe that this event has shaped your choices later in life? How so?

_____

_____

_____

_____

What do you remember about Job's hardships? What did he lose? How did he react?

_____

_____

_____

_____

Have you become obsessed with seeking revenge from your past hurt? Do you feel that it is important that everyone know about your past hurts and how they affected you?

_____

_____

_____

_____

Do you find yourself speaking about those events on a regular basis?

_____

_____

_____

_____

PRAYER:

Lord, please reveal to me areas of my past that I have not given to you. I do not want to live in the past. I do not want my past to consume me. Allow me to deal with this pain so that I can become the woman and mother that you want me to be. Amen.

PLAYING THE VICTIM ROLE
WEEK 5

Do you find that you are extremely hard on yourself? Do you say things like, "I am too fat. I am not pretty enough. My children never obey me. I am not a good mom."

_____

_____

_____

_____

Think of someone who has suffered tremendously in their life. Write their story here.

_____

_____

_____

_____

Is there someone who has less money than you? Poorer health? Begin to thank God for what you have. List some of your blessings here.

_____

_____

_____

_____

Have you ever wondered why you have suffered such hardships in your life? Write Isaiah 55:8–9 here.

_____

_____

_____

_____

Record Romans 8:28 here. Does this give you a new perspective on your past?

_____

_____

_____

_____

PRAYER:

Father, help me to be thankful for who I am and what I have. Help me to not focus on what I have suffered in my past. Keep me focused on my positive future. Amen.

CHAPTER 10
PARENTING 101

Every mom wants to be able to say, "I am very proud of my son/daughter." We want to watch our children graduate high school with honors, as the star athlete, and then move on to college. We want them to become doctors and marry the perfect person. We envision the best for our children, far more than we ever had. Even if you provide the best parenting you possibly can, there is no guarantee that your child will become all those things listed above. We do, however, want to do our best in helping Little Sally or Little Johnny achieve their best.

Proverbs 31:27–28 says, "She carefully watches everything in her household and suffers nothing to laziness. Her children stand and bless her."

Oh, to hear my children stand and bless me one day! What an honor as a mom. We all should aspire to such a blessing. Did you read what the first part of that verse says? She is not lazy. Good parenting takes effort. It is not easy. It is not free, but it is worth it.

How could I write a guide for the single mom and not discuss parenting? You could go to the local bookstore and purchase every parenting book available and still not have all the tools necessary to raise your child. Spank them. Don't spank them. Give them bedtime at eight o'clock p.m. Wait until ten o'clock p.m. Many books contradict each other. Perhaps you read through my advice and do not agree with all of it. But the following information is what I have found to be the most effective parenting skills for single mothers, based on my own experience, biblical teachings, and years of working with other single moms.

I have taught parenting classes to single moms for years now. Brace yourself for this one. I do not consider myself to be an expert. Most authors would never say such a thing. But this statement raises to mind the following question. Who is a parenting expert? How do you get that title? A PhD from Harvard? Perhaps. I, personally, would rather have coffee with a group of experienced mothers and discuss what they have found is working and what does not work with rearing children. I would rather listen to a grandmother who has successfully raised five productive children facilitate a round-table discussion on the subject. That is what this segment will be; what I believe works, based on my own experience, teaching and counseling, and God's Word. Envision me sitting with you having a discussion on your living room sofa. This is real talk for real moms.

Ladies, it is time for a gut check. The fact that you are reading this book tells me you are looking for help and a way to grow as a single mother. Now is the time for self-reflection. You need to ask yourself some pretty tough questions that you may not like the answers to. Give yourself a few minutes to reflect on the following:

1. Do I have a relationship with Jesus? Do I understand what that means? Can I pinpoint a time in my life when I gave my life to the Lord?

2. Do I feel good enough? Do I feel worthy of love?

3. Am I happy where I am right now?

4. Do I believe that God put dreams inside of me? Am I taking steps to realize and live out those dreams?

The answer to all those questions must be an emphatic, "Yes!" If not, then you need to begin to work through each area that isn't. For example, since having a relationship with Christ is the key to having joy, peace, love, and patience, how can you effectively parent without a relationship with him? Don't you need those things to parent? What about being happy with who you are, and feeling good enough? If the answer is no, then you will have a hard time imparting positive wisdom to your child. You have to work through those issues that prevent you from feeling good enough or that prevent you from dreaming of your future successes.

Let me explain it to you this way. As a single mom, you are super-busy. You could be attending school, working, or doing both. You may be working multiple jobs. In addition, you are caring for your child who has school projects, basketball practice, and a doctor's appointment. You are extremely busy with many things, and worrying about you is the last thing you should be doing, right? Wrong. The first step to effectively parenting your child is working on you. Just look at the emotional scars that many of us have suffered through based on our parents' mistakes in parenting, their inadequacies. If you are not a whole person (well-rounded, full of joy, and optimistic), then the task of parenting alone will almost be more than you can bear. Life does not stop when you become a mom, so continue to work on yourself.

Once you have begun to work on you, both emotionally and spiritually, then we can move on to some parenting do's and don'ts. When I began to think about starting a single mom's ministry, my initial reason for wanting to start it was to give parenting advice. Quite frankly, I had seen one too many ill-behaved children. While my own parenting has not been flawless, by a long shot, I am thankful to have raised well-behaved, respectful, successful children. I want to help other women do the same, if I can.

As I began the journey of working with women, I uncovered four common parenting mistakes:

1. Overindulgence out of guilt. This is a scary one. This is the most common of the four. Mom wants her child to be happy. She wants to do everything in her power to make that happen. Oftentimes, she feels guilty that somehow it may be her fault that Dad does not live with them or her fault that she chose Dad in the first place, so she caters to the child's every whim. Have you ever seen a child fall to the floor in the toy aisle of the local discount store, screaming and kicking because he wants the latest toy truck? Embarrassed, Mom leans over and quietly whispers, "Johnny, if you will calm down, then we will get the truck." Johnny gets up with a smile on his face as he walks away with the toy in his hand. Have you ever been that mom? I sure have!

I have seen moms that are having serious financial difficulty purchase their children all the latest name-brand fashions, expensive electronic equipment (such as iPods , gaming devices, and cell phones), or throw them extravagant parties. This is done from guilt, guilt that she doesn't have the money to provide the same as Sally's parents, guilt that her child doesn't have a dad around, or guilt that the Jones family down the street is doing it.

Parents, in general, have this problem. I wouldn't be honest to tell you that I have never over-indulged one of my children. However, with single moms, it escalates ten-fold because there is no one else there to help balance out a poor parenting decision. You want your child to feel loved, and you become overcome with that desire, not realizing the negative implications. What is the result of such over-indulgence? Everyone knows about that spoiled-rotten kid from the neighborhood, or the smart-mouthed teenager that everyone avoids. That is the result. You will be raising that child. Constantly indulging your child's wants, whether money is an issue or not, leads to a lack of respect between you and your child. You become the ATM, not the parent.

Be strong. Do not give in. Your child will grow up ill-prepared for life if you always give in.

2. Failing to discipline. There are several reasons that a single mom fails to discipline her child. Exhaustion comes to mind, as that was surely part of my own struggle. After carrying the weight of the world on your shoulders all day, it is much easier to just give in than to listen to them ask a dozen times or listen to a temper tantrum. Another reason for failing to discipline is fear of being the constant bad guy. Because you do not have the luxury of a second parent that can sometimes be the disciplinarian, you always must do it. You may want your child to love you, and it's hard to watch them be angry at you when you discipline. Lastly, many moms are unsure of how to discipline, so they simply do not do it. They are afraid of making mistakes or duplicating their own childhood, so they become immobile. Whatever the reason, you must discipline. Remember you are not your child's friend. You are his parent.

Your child craves structure and discipline from a very young age. Anything less than that leads to rowdy, disrespectful children. You give your child the gift of love, security, and belonging when you discipline, and that is what true love is all about.

3. Being too strict leads to rebellion. Wow, have I struggled with this one! While you certainly do not want to be the pushover parent, there is a line that you do not want to cross into being too strict. Parental instruction should be given for protection and growth opportunities for your child. Be careful not to abuse your authority by becoming a bully. Because you cannot control that your rent is two months behind or that your ex-husband is not paying child support on time, it is easy to relay that frustration to your child. When you cannot control other things in your life, it is natural to want to control those things that you can. This method will backfire and usually leads to rebellious, confrontational children in the future.

Here is an example. My dad was a huge disciplinarian. He was too strict in many areas. He screened every phone call. Our bedtime was nine o'clock p.m. as high school students. He prohibited boys from calling our house (even as high school seniors)! We were never allowed to date. What did I do as a result? I began to sneak around behind his back and do it anyway. At seventeen years old, I was pregnant, yet I still could not date or have conversations on the phone with boys. Boys were the enemy in my dad's world. Rather than educating me about the proper behavior with them. He secluded me. His attempts backfired. Yours will, too.

4. Negatively impacting your child's character. Growing up, my dad would say to me, "Don't do as I do; do as I say do." Many parents still use that same approach today. After years of watching my dad in sexual immorality, is it any wonder that I began that same pattern? Moms, it is not good enough to merely tell your child not to engage in certain activities, you must be an example. It is important to first consider what type of character you want to develop in your child. When you think of a man or woman of high integrity, what words come to mind? Moral. Honest. Kind. Pure.

Your child is watching your every move. Ask yourself a simple question. "Would I want my child doing what I am doing right now?" This is an accurate gauge of how effective you are at being a good example for your child to follow. Do not think that your toddler or young child does not notice what you are doing. I have memories as early as two years old, as do most people.

There are dozens of areas where your child is watching you. I chose to name a few here:

- Sex. You are not fooling your child when you say, "Mr. Bob and Mom are going to have a slumber party, tonight." They instinctively know something is wrong. They may not be able to articulate it yet, but they know.

- Music, Internet, and television. Do you watch questionable television programs with foul language or illicit sex? Do you listen to music of the same description? What you feed your spirit becomes embedded in your thoughts. Would you want your child to repeat verbatim the movie you just watched? If not, cut it out of your life.

- Honesty. When you find $20 in the parking lot, turn it back into the grocery store manager. Do not reason that you really need the money. When you want cable television, do not run a wire from your neighbor's house. Buy your own or do without it. However minor these examples may seem, they provide excellent opportunities for you to increase your child's integrity. Do the right thing, even when it is difficult.

- Prejudices. Whether we are talking about racism, sexism, or economic status, we absolutely want our children to be free of such prejudices. Be careful not to categorize others based on the references listed above, but rather by the condition of their heart. If this is an area you struggle in, begin to pray that the Lord would give you a new way of thinking. Release any bitterness you have against another race or gender.

If someone says, I love God, but hates a Christian brother or sister, that person is a liar; for if we don't love people we can see, how can we love God, whom we cannot see? And He has given us this command: Those who love God must also love their Christian brothers and sisters.

1 John 4:20–21

Now that we have discussed some of the parenting mistakes, let us begin to discuss five ways to make you a better mom.

Step one is to recognize that you need help. You cannot do it alone. Yes, you are a single mom, but you must begin to lean on family and friends for occasional help. Do not be prideful. None of us can do it fully alone.

> Two people are better off than one, for they can help each other succeed. If one person falls, the other can reach out and help. But someone who falls alone is in real trouble. Likewise, two people lying together can keep warm. But how can one be warm alone? A person standing alone can be attacked and defeated, but two can stand back to back and conquer. Three are even better, for a triple-braided cord is not easily broken.
>
> Ecclesiastes 4:9–12

That is a pretty straightforward approach. Reach out to each other for help. Join a mom's playgroup. Join a Sunday school class. Start a Single Mom's Dinner Club to meet once a month. Form a babysitting co-op with other area moms.

Step two is allowing yourself some alone time. This is imperative. I know that it may not seem like a big issue, but it is. You must have time to regroup, when your world does not revolve around your children. There has to be quiet prayer time. For some, this may be a long bath after the kids are in bed. For others, you may awake before the children and get some quiet time in your room. Twice a month, take time to meet with a friend, counselor, or mentor. If babysitting is an issue, use the babysitting co-op mentioned in step one.

Step three is talking to your kids. From the time your infant is born, begin to talk to him. Sing to him. Praise him. As children grow, they need verbal affirmation from their parents. No subject is off-limits as they become older. Sex, financial matters, personal hygiene, and spiritual growth need desperately to be taught in the home first. All of these things are discussed at school and with friends. You do not want the drug dealer at a local convenient store to be the first one to discuss drugs with your child. Be bold. Open the door of communication very early and keep it open.

If you now have a teenager and you have not had an open line of communication, start now. It may be awkward at first, but keep working at it. Do not give up no matter what your teen's reaction. Start with an apology. "Sally, I am sorry that I have not talked with you as much as I should have through the years. I have let life get in the way. I have let my hurt over other things distract me. I love you. I want to begin our relationship again. Will you forgive me?" With persistence, this approach will pay off. It shows your teen that you are not above an apology and you care about them.

Avoid using foul language or screaming at your child. If you feel your anger beginning to rise to that point, walk away immediately. Your child's self-esteem is ripped down every time you scream. Be careful not to start this trend. Remember, they are watching.

Step four—dream. Do not allow life to beat you down to a point where you forget your dreams. We all have hopes, aspirations, and dreams. Sometimes, we are too scared to begin to talk about them again because we have suffered many disappointments in the past. We fear future rejection. You have a purpose. You may have dreamed of becoming a hairdresser or opening your own daycare center. You may desire to get a college degree so that you can teach school. Go for it. Stop listening to the negative thoughts and fears from the past. Jump into the new thing God has for you, the exciting thing.

Jeremiah 29:11 says, "For I know the plans I have for you, says the Lord. They are plans for good and not for disaster, to give you a future and a hope."

The best thing you can do for your children's dreams is achieve your own. You never want your son or daughter to look back and wonder why Mom never opened that restaurant she always dreamed about. Whatever your dream, it is achievable. There are many government agencies that assist in funding education for low-income families or provide childcare, so that you may pursue your dream. Non-profit organizations and churches all over the country have programs set up to help you start on your path.

Your children have dreams as well. Be an encourager. Foster an environment that allows your children to thrive. Build up your children by speaking positivity over them. Tell them they can do anything.

Step five is to change your community. Volunteer. It is such a rewarding experience.

Maybe you are barely holding on to your apartment right now, as they are threatening eviction. Then go to the local homeless shelter and serve. Pray over their needs. If you have just been given a bad medical diagnosis, go to a local hospital or nursing home to visit with others. Although I have suffered tremendous abuse, it took me less than twenty-four hours of volunteering in a battered woman's shelter to realize that my abuse paled in comparison to the travesties some women have endured. Volunteering offers a new perspective. There is always someone that is worse off than you. There is always someone to serve. Volunteering takes your mind off your own problems and allows you to reach out to others.

Remember how we talked about developing your child's character? What better way than through giving back to the community could you teach him or her about integrity? When you think about wanting to have your son or daughter marry the perfect person for them, begin to develop them into the perfect mate for that future spouse.

Think about babysitting for a friend. Cook dinner for an elderly neighbor. Run errands for a widow. Bake cookies for the apartment building. Fold clothes for a neighbor. There are thousands of low-cost ways to serve.

As you can see, the name of the game is a balanced life. The more well rounded you are, the better chance you are giving your children for a successful life. Through all the mistakes we make, we learn and grow. Do not spend time worrying about your past. Do not dwell on your inadequacies. Don't worry that your child doesn't live in a large, two-story home with a white picket fence around the backyard.

The life you lead may not be the one you envisioned for yourself or your children. That is okay. Embrace where you are right now. Enjoy your children. Enjoy who God made you to be and trust that you have been given these children to raise because God knows you can do it and do it well.

PARENTING 101
WEEK 6

What is your primary goal as a mother? Do you effectively communicate that to your children through words and actions?

_____

_____

_____

_____

There are four common parenting mistakes that single mothers make. What are they?

_____

_____

_____

_____

Which parenting mistake do you most closely identify with?

_____

_____

_____

_____

How can you begin to work on that area of your parenting?

_____

_____

_____

_____

What is your number one fear as a parent?

_____

_____

_____

_____

Are there things in your life that you do that you would never want your child to do? How can you prevent your child from doing them?

_____

_____

_____

_____

PRAYER:

Lord, I want to be the best mom I can possibly be. Help me to use wisdom with my parenting. Help me to be sensitive to my child's needs without becoming too lenient. Help me to raise my child up to be all you have called him to be. Amen.

PARENTING 101
WEEK 7

As a single parent, you must have help. Read Ephesians 4:9–12. Who in your life can you lean on to help with parenting?

_____

_____

_____

_____

Alone time is crucial in parenting. Do not allow yourself to feel guilty about having that time. What in the last time you had complete alone time? What can you do to get regular alone time?

_____

_____

_____

_____

Do you talk to your children on a regular basis, other than giving them instructions? Why or why not?

_____

_____

_____

_____

Write down a dream you have for your future. What does Jeremiah 29:11 say about your future?

_____

_____

_____

_____

List ways that you can volunteer in your community with your children. How do you think volunteering will make you feel about yourself?

_____

_____

_____

_____

PRAYER:

Heavenly Father, help me to foster friendships with people that can help me to effectively parent my children. Do not allow me to be prideful. I will accept the help, when it is offered. Help me to begin to dream again about my future and the future of my children. Thank you that you are changing me from the inside out.

CHAPTER 11

SURVIVING FINANCIAL CRISIS

I awoke one morning and began my morning routine. I showered and dressed. I brushed my teeth, and then reached for my contact lenses. I opened the container and accidentally ripped the lens in half with my fingernail. Since this was years before disposable lenses were popular, I did not have a replacement pair. I reached for my old glasses that were fitted with an expired prescription. Although they were the size of my grandmother's glasses, which covered half my face and I could barely see with them, they would have to do.

I cried all the way to work that morning. As I sat at my desk crying, my boss came in and asked, "What's wrong?"

I began to cry uncontrollably. Through tears, I muttered, "I ripped my contact lens this morning and I do not have the money to replace it, so I had to wear this ugly pair of glasses. Tomorrow is my daughter's second birthday, and I do not have the money for that either. And to top it all off, my car is acting up."

He paused for a moment and then asked, "Is there anything else going on?"

Puzzled, I said, "No. Isn't that enough?" I knew that he did not understand. I did not mean that I was struggling a little and that funds were low. I meant that there was no money, none. There was not some rainy day fund hiding away in the mattress somewhere. I had no emergency money for when the car broke down or the refrigerator was acting up. There was not a 401k account that I could borrow from temporarily. I mean, I had to count pennies to put $1.08 gas in my car to get to work. My boss was a wealthy business owner who came from a family of influence. He was a kind and compassionate boss, but I knew he did not understand the depths of my poverty or what it did to me emotionally.

With all my other troubles, it seemed financial burden was just one more thing added to my shoulders. I was doing everything I could to keep my head above water financially, but it seemed to never be good enough. I was tired of being so frugal with my money and still not having enough. I was exhausted with doing it all on my own. Would it ever get any better?

Many of you have probably heard 2 Timothy 6:10 which says, "For the love of money is the root of all kinds of evil." It sure seemed evil when the landlord came for my rent every month! Obviously, we need money to function, but we want to be careful that we do not cross the line of loving it, and all it stands for. In some ways, I equate money to food. We need it to survive. It is important, but when we start loving it, there are consequences to follow.

There was a time in my life when I was obsessed with money. It was all I could think about. I was going to college to earn more money. I worked extra hours to have extra money. *If I only had more money, life would not be so difficult,* I thought. And there is some truth to that. Of course, life is easier when you do not have to spend time wondering where your next meal is coming from, or how you will pay your car note. I agree. What I did not realize at that time, though, was even if someone threw millions of dollars at me, it still would not have been enough to make me happy.

Isn't it ironic that when some of the most successful Hollywood actors are interviewed by magazines or television reporters, their responses are often similar? They seldom speak of their overwhelming happiness. In fact, many of them speak about loneliness, depression, drug addiction, and failed marriages. Yet, many of us spend our lives in pursuit of an extravagant lifestyle with an overflow of financial wealth similar to that of a movie star.

The Bible does not say that money is evil. It is a necessity for us to function in society and be productive at what we have been called to do. It is the love of money that is evil. Jesus says in Matthew 6:24, "No one can serve two masters. For you will hate one and love the other; you will be devoted to one and despise the other. You cannot serve both God and money." He is not saying you cannot serve God if you have money, but rather it cannot be the master of your life, your focus, or source of happiness.

Having said all that, you still have bills to pay, groceries to purchase, and children to send to school. All of which cost money. The next several pages are designed to help you work through your financial difficulties with simple tips and direction. Because single moms vary in age, experience, and financial circumstances, I want to start with the very basics of money.

Part of my financial woes early in life was ignorance. We had only a modest income growing up. No one had taught me about how to open a checking account, much less balance one. I did not know much about budgeting or credit bureaus. These things were all equivalent to a foreign language. Most high schools do not offer classes that specifically cover money basics. If you do not learn it at home and it is not offered in school, where do you learn about finances? I know that is where some of you are. If you were never taught, then you are flying blind. You simply do not know. This chapter is designed to help you know.

TITHING

When I transitioned from my late teens to early twenties, I had hit rock bottom. I was working a job with no potential for promotion, raising two children on food stamps and welfare, with no end in sight. I had supported my children, at one point, on approximately $400 per month. The next job I took doubled my income, and I was making approximately $900 per month, which was wonderful to me, but still not enough to get off government assistance.

This is when the principle of tithing was re-introduced into my life through a sermon at church. As I said earlier, I had grown up attending church, and I am sure I had heard about tithing. However, I did not remember much. After hearing this particular sermon on tithing, I wrestled for some time with the concept. *How am I supposed to give the church my money when I can barely pay my bills?* I would think. Though I had my reservations, I could not get it off my mind, so I just did it.

Tithing may be new to you, so let me introduce it, here.

> Then, Abram gave Melchizedek a tenth of all the goods he had recovered (Genesis 14:20).

> One tenth of the produce of the land, whether grain from the fields or fruit from the trees, belongs to the Lord and must be set apart to him as holy. (Leviticus 27:30).

> You must set aside of your crops—one-tenth of all crops you harvest each year. (Deuteronomy 14:22).

> Bring all the tithes into the storehouse so there will be enough food in my temple. "If you do,' says the Lord of Heaven's Armies, 'I will open the windows of heaven for you. I will pour out a blessing so great you won't have enough room to take it in! Try it! Put me to the test' (Malachi 3:10).

From the beginning of scripture, we are instructed to give ten percent of our increase to God. That means, if you receive $500 weekly, you give $50 to God through your local church. Here is where it can get real tricky for us. Some of the thoughts I had (and you may be having) were, "I cannot afford to do this. That sure seems like a great deal of my money. I bet the pastor wants a pay raise or a new car!"

> And don't give reluctantly or in response to pressure. For God loves a person who gives cheerfully. And God will generously provide all you need. Then, you will always have everything you need and plenty left over to share with others.
>
> 2 Corinthians 9:7–8

First, the Lord calls us to be cheerful in our giving. He calls us to give only ten percent, while leaving us in control of the other ninety. It is all his anyway. This is not because God needs our money. All heaven and earth belong to him. This is a test of our faith and obedience. As for the pastor needing a pay raise or a new car, God commanded the tithe. Your pastor did not come up with the idea. Some pastors even avoid speaking on the subject for fear the congregation may think such thoughts. If it is true and funds are being misused, let God deal with that. This does not relieve you of your obligation to tithe.

Lastly, do not think you cannot afford to tithe. You cannot afford not to! As seen in the scriptures listed, the Lord is telling us to try him. He will provide all our needs and pour out blessings on us.

As I released the fears about tithing, I became faithful in my giving. I never looked back. I began to experience financial freedom in its fullest. Within months of tithing, I landed a new job, for which I was not qualified, in my opinion. I began earning more than one thousand times my prior annual income. How does that happen? It was not that I no longer had bills. I simply no longer worried about them. I knew God was going to provide. I did not worry about how or when, because I stood on that truth of knowing he would, in his perfect timing. I got off food stamps and moved from government housing. I was finally able to purchase a car that did not leave me stranded on the roadside regularly.

It is important for me to stop and note that God is not our magical genie. We do not rub on the lamp and begin making demands. The same is true for tithing, attending church, or reading your Bible. Those are all great things that we should do, but they are not tools used to barter with God. He will provide what we need and sometimes what we want in his timing, when it is best for us, not when we demand it, through a desperate prayer.

I spent several years making more money than I could have ever hoped for or imagined. I vacationed in exotic locations. I took a cruise. I ate in fine dining establishments. I purchased a large home and a nice automobile. Those were all things that I believe the Lord blessed me with through my obedience to tithe. However, that is not where the story ended. There came a time in my life several years later when the Lord tested my obedience, once again. He called me to leave my position as a successful executive and volunteer full time with single moms. I would love to tell you that I dropped everything and immediately obeyed. I did not.

After over a year of contemplating how we would make it financially, I finally obeyed. The Lord gently reminded me that he was my provider and while my company had been a blessing to me, it was not my source. It was now time to move on to a new season of my life, leaving behind the things of old—money and all. I jumped into ministry with both feet, working with single mothers, having coffee with them, doing lunch, and praying with them. I began doing speaking engagements, all for free. Not once has a bill been unpaid in my home. This new season has given me the opportunity to be more resourceful in my spending, more conscious of what I spend, and to learn more about discounts and coupons. All of those things have allowed my ministry to flourish more. Those were things that single moms needed to know, so God allowed me to learn first.

BUDGETING

Now that you understand tithing, let's talk about budgets. Budgeting is another necessity in money management for the single mom. Many of us were not reared in lavish surroundings, so it should come as no surprise that adding children into a single-parent household will require some belt-tightening.

It is imperative, whether you are recently divorced or newly expecting, that you have a budget. The first step in budgeting is to know exactly what income enters the home and what leaves it. The easiest way to track this is via a check register, so I recommend opening a checking account. Be sure you inquire about a free checking account, as most banks now offer them. (This may seem like an obvious thing to do - to have a checking account - but believe it or not, many women do not have one or have never opened their own.) When you begin receiving monthly checking account statements, be sure to balance them (review your statement to match it against your check register ensuring totals match).

After opening a checking account, the second step to budgeting is to list on paper every bill you owe. This includes: housing, utilities, car notes, insurance, food, gas, school expenses, and any others that remain unnamed. Some expenses may need to be estimated, such as gas or food, until you begin to know what you spend every month. List debtors by payment, balance, and interest rate. A sample list is below:

	MONTHLY OBLIGATION	BALANCE	INTEREST RATE
Mortgage note	$800	$100,000	9%
Car	$400	$12,000	12%
Credit Card	$25	$500	21%
Department store	$10	$300	28%
Daycare	$400		
Utilities	$400		
Gas	$300		
TOTAL	$2,335/ month		

For the next thirty days, list every penny you spend on paper. If you buy a cup of coffee, list it. Nothing goes under the radar. Be diligent. At the end of the thirty days, sit down and assess your financial situation. Did anything surprise you? Are you spending more on gas than you anticipated? Have you bought more magazines or coffee than you bargained for?

Some important items to note when tracking your income are as follows. Number one: be sure to count food stamps, welfare checks, or government rental assistance as income, if applicable. However, do not count bonuses, commissions, or sporadic child support. These are less predictable forms of income and should never be counted on, but rather viewed as a blessing once received.

I have counseled hundreds of people through financial crisis. The one thing that always surprises me is even though someone recognizes that they are having financial difficulty, they still do not have a budget on paper and oftentimes do not know what they owe. This is a must. You cannot begin to improve your finances if you do not know exactly where you are with them.

Let's start by comparing your list of monthly obligations to what you actually spent in the last thirty days. Are there some things not listed on your monthly obligations? Of course, there are. We all make purchases that we are not obligated to make, but rather, we choose to make. For example, we are obligated to pay the rent or we will have nowhere to live. However, we are not obligated to go to the movies with our best girlfriend on Friday night. This is when priorities begin to change.

Do not stop with the thirty-day evaluation. Keep a notebook or running total of all income and expenses. You will begin to accurately assess how much you need for groceries, gas, and diapers. This allows you to more closely budget what you can afford to spend on each. Speaking of what you can afford, now is time to introduce a new word: over-spending!

No one wants to hear this word, but we all need to. Let me explain to you the difference between needs and wants. Needs are food, housing, transportation, clothing, diapers, and toiletries. You need to pay for insurance or gas. Those are all needs. Wants are manicures, haircuts, eyebrow waxes, movie nights, restaurant expenses, and new clothes, shoes that are on clearance, and anything else that you do not absolutely have to have to survive. Clothing is listed under needs and wants. Let me clarify. You need to have clothing to go to work in. You do not need to visit the mall because they are having a sale on all the latest fashions. That is a want.

Transportation is a necessity. You must be able to get your children to school and you need a way to work. Whether you are using public transportation or have your own car, you must budget for such an expense. However, you do not need a new BMW. You may want one. They may look great, but you cannot justify it. Manicures? "Oh, but you do not know what my nails look like if I do not have a professional take care of them," you may say. Haircuts? Do you get your hair cut at the top salon in town or at the local Budget Cuts down the street? Yes, I know Bob at the salon has done your hair for years, but you may no longer be able to afford him. Do not misunderstand. We all enjoy getting special treatments and purchasing new clothes. However, when your budget is extremely tight, you cannot justify the purchase of that new outfit, no matter what percentage it was marked down on the clearance rack.

This may seem like such a simple concept for many of

you. I hope it is. But for many others, it is a huge struggle. I have had countless single moms approach the ministry and ask for assistance with their finances, but when I further evaluate their situation, they have chosen to not scale back their way of living. We find a lifestyle that we are comfortable with, but when life changes, we change with it. Your budget may no longer afford you the opportunity for that daily cup of coffee at the local bistro. The purchase of diapers may be your new obligation. This is when we must tell our children "no" to the huge birthday extravaganza or the new outfit. Perhaps, they cannot join in a particular activity at this time. That is okay. You are teaching them responsibility. Accept it now and you will have a much smoother transition.

As you begin to eliminate some unnecessary expenditure from your life, you will find that budgeting is much easier. Maybe you spent $4 per day on coffee. This would equate to $120 per month or perhaps you saved $30 by purchasing your shoes at the thrift store versus the mall. Every dollar saved can be reallocated, no matter how small it may seem.

Where do we apply these newfound funds? Refer to your budget again. Do you remember how I asked you to list interest rates of all debt owed, including balances? Begin to apply whatever extra you have found in your budget to that debt. You will never have financial freedom when you are drowning in debtors. This leads to our next topic.

CREDIT BUREAU REPORT

I still find it ironic that in my early twenties, I was counseling people about their finances, when I was living on food stamps and welfare. God certainly has a sense of humor, doesn't he? Credit Bureau Reports were one of those things that I learned about early in my financial counseling career. I can remember wondering why no one had shared this information with me before and how people functioned financially when they did not fully understand how their credit report worked. The sad thing is that many people ruin their credit report in their late teens and early twenties, before they even understand how it works.

Credit Reports are used in several areas of life. Most people know that they are used to assess your credit worthiness by a lender for future lending for items such as homes and automobiles, as well as personal loans. However, were you aware that your credit bureau can also be pulled in conjunction with an application for employment? Did you know that many landlords will not rent to a tenant without a copy of the tenant's credit bureau? Automobile and homeowner's insurance companies often require a credit report to be pulled.

As you can see, your credit report follows you for the rest of your life and in many areas that you perhaps never thought about.

Psalm 37:20 offers interesting insight into what the Bible says about debt. "The wicked borrow and never repay, but the godly are generous givers." The Bible is very clear about what our responsibilities are to our lenders.

"But what if my current credit situation is not my

fault?" you may ask. That is an unfortunate situation that many of you may find yourselves in. Maybe you allowed your ex-husband to pay all the bills and handle financial matters for your home. Perhaps an ex-boyfriend abused your kindness and used your credit cards to acquire debt you were not aware of, or left you holding the bag with payments. Maybe you co-signed for a friend who never paid the debt.

First of all, let us use the above-mentioned scenarios as learning experiences. At no time should either spouse have sole control over the finances. This prevents an unexpected death from leaving one spouse clueless. It also allows both spouses to pray about financial matters together. Single moms are much more susceptible to the other scenarios, particularly as it relates to boyfriends. Sometimes, single moms have given so much of themselves to caring for their children that at the end of the day they want to be hugged and feel that they are being taken care of.

It is when this desire is at its highest and the guard is down that we can sometimes be manipulated into co-signing for a boyfriend who does not have acceptable credit or even lending credit cards for a charge that he promises he will pay. Both examples are recipes for disaster. Ask yourself the obvious questions. "Why doesn't he have acceptable credit, if he always pays his lender on time? If he is going to pay me back, why can't he just save for the item and purchase it at a later time?" Moms, guard yourselves. Do not allow your emotions to entangle you in a financial catastrophe. Ultimately, you are responsible for any purchases made in your name.

There are three things that I have often seen as the cause for unsatisfactory credit ratings. First, individuals over-estimate their ability to repay based on what they perceive their financial status is versus what it really is. For example, you run out and buy the new dress at the local department store because it is on sale and Little Johnny's kindergarten graduation is coming up. You charge it on a credit card and say, in passing, "I get paid next Friday. I'll just pay it off then." Inevitably, five other things come up, and before you know it, there are dozens of small purchases made that are sitting on credit cards that you simply cannot pay. Do you remember me discussing over-spending?

Secondly, individuals are hit with unexpected medical expenses. If you are reading this and have never had a medical emergency, be aware that it can financially ruin you! Please purchase medical insurance and make preparations for medical emergencies in a savings account. It is not a luxury. Most employers now offer health insurance. Do not decline that option. Another option is government assistance, which some of you may qualify for. If neither of those options is available, pursue a local insurance agent and find out what your options are.

The last most common reason for unsatisfactory credit ratings is divorce. Many of you find yourselves there today. You were unaware of the family's financial situation. You entrusted your ex-husband to take care of those things and he did not. Or, maybe you both overspent, over-estimated your ability to pay, and did not save for a rainy day. Whatever the reasons for your credit situation, we must now deal with it.

Obtain a copy of your credit report. You are entitled to a free one every year. They are easily ordered on-line. Once received, begin to contact creditors that you have not paid. If you charged a credit card when you were eighteen and never paid it, you still owe the debt. Make it right. Begin to diligently work with each creditor to repay your debts. The same is true for medical bills. If you can only afford $10 per month, then make that offer to the lender. If you must use income tax returns to pay the debt, do it. Do not make plans for new purchases with extra money you receive, until you have diligently paid every lender what is due. This is what is right. Remember. You are teaching your children integrity. I caution you in not becoming bitter about paying a debtor that was an ex-spouse or ex-boyfriend's responsibility. If the debt is on your credit, pay it. Do not waste any more time hoping that he will do what is right. It will not help your credit situation. And you can use it as an opportunity to teach your children character.

It takes a time to begin to repair a poor credit report. You must pay the debts. Your credit scores will not change overnight. But the daunting task of detangling your credit problems will not go away, so begin today.

COUPONS AND DISCOUNTS

This is an area that has been a true adventure for me through the years. As you will remember, I went from making a substantial amount of income to volunteering and make $0 annually for quite some time. I was working full-time on a volunteer basis. With my husband now as the sole provider of our family's income, I decided to become creative with our income and thus, I was introduced to coupons.

In Matthew 25:14–30, Jesus shares the parable of the loaned money. Three servants were given money by their master and made choices about how to handle the money. One servant invested his money and doubled it. Another servant went to work and doubled his money as well. However, the last servant buried his money in the ground, fearing he would lose the money. The story ends with this dramatic conclusion in Matthew 25:29. "To those who use well what they are given, even more will be given, and they will have an abundance. But from those who do nothing, even what little they have will be taken away."

We are all called to be good stewards of what we are blessed with. Finances may be extremely difficult for you right now. But, hold on. You be faithful. You continue to be diligent with your tithing, paying your debtors, and stretching your budget to its fullest. There will be a new season for you. I do not know when, but I know that Malachi 3:10 promises you favor. When I entered the world of coupons and discounts, I knew that was exactly what God was teaching me; to be a good steward with what I had. Because of what I have learned, I now know that I will not go back to spending more than necessary for groceries or toiletries. That is money that I can use to bless a single mom, or sow into our church ministries, or serve a homeless meal.

I have heard countless single mothers tell me that they simply did not have the time to clip coupons or that they did not know where to begin. Let me first tell you that with the new organizational information available on the web, you do not have to clip them until you need them. Watching your favorite television program while clipping coupons doesn't seem so bad if I tell you that you could save as much as 90% on your grocery budget, does it?

Many moms are unaware of all the discounts available. First, let me tell you that coupons should become your best friend. Do not pay full price. There are coupons for restaurants, movie theaters, and groceries. Begin to purchase your Sunday paper. Begin to print coupons from the Internet. Follow blogs and websites that highlight savings in your local area. Free samples are available from every major discount store in America and can be accessed at their websites. I once used free shampoo samples for over thirty days when funds were limited on the family's toiletry budget for the month!

Major drug store and grocery retailers, such as Walgreens, CVS, Rite-Aid, Winn-Dixie, Albertsons, offer discounts, bonuses, and reward points to frequent shoppers. Many of these stores even offer rebate programs that allow for free items every month.

Begin to think about the amount of money you spend on food, soap, diapers, cleaning products, and toilet paper. It adds up to significant amounts of money. If you can get many of those items for free or at discounts of up to 90%, would you consider spending some designated time every month researching the savings?

Stephanie Nelson is The Coupon Mom and hosts the website www.thecouponmom.com. Since 2004, she has appeared on Good Morning America, The Oprah Winfrey Show, The Today Show, and countless others. She shares her secrets and tips on how to save on everything. Her website will provide you with detailed information on how to get started. She offers a free e Book called *Cut Your Grocery Bill in Half with the Coupon Mom System* at www.coolsavings.com. Her website provides a chat forum where you can ask questions and chat with other frugal moms. She provides free information on coupons, restaurant savings, discounts, rebates, free samples, and holiday and back to school savings. Hers is just one of many blogs, websites, and apps available for review and download.

When I began using coupons and discounts, as well as rebate programs, I saved hundreds of dollars for my family. I saved $400 monthly just by using coupons and strategically watching for sales at local grocery stores. I began to carpool with friends when necessary. I began to plan my weekly trips to the market and post office so that they coincided with other errands to save on gas. I used store brand products when feasible. I became diligent about turning lights off around the house or not having our air conditioning system cooling too low in our home. Every area of our finances where I could cut back, I did. Eventually, I saved our family over $1,000 monthly by making only simple changes. You can, too. Search the Web. There are thousands of websites and blogs now available to help with money savings. Search for books and magazines with money-saving tips. There are dozens of television shows that offer great tips for the frugal parent. In addition, many churches are now offering coupon classes to help others save and budget. So, get started.

EMOTIONS

Discussing money evokes many emotions. I understand. Some of you continue to deal with feelings of inadequacy or failure. You feel that you have failed in a marriage, failed as a mother, and failed at finances. Now, you are entrusted to raise a child alone. You feel ill equipped for such a mighty task. You have not had much experience with handling finances and fear failure in that area as well.

I encourage you with this word. 2 Timothy 1:7 says, "For God has not given us a spirit of fear and timidity, but of power, love, and self-discipline."

You do not have to fear your finances. Do not let past failures determine your future action. This verse tells us that he has equipped you with power—yes, power. He has equipped you with love, and then, there is self-discipline. You have already shown great discipline to get this book and begin to change your life. Maybe you are even part of a single mom Bible study. The challenge will now be for you to become self-disciplined with your spending and budgeting habits. There is no doubt that you can.

As you finish this chapter, I pray that you begin to feel hope. I want you to be excited about what you are learning as a single mom. I want you to embark on each new area of your life with hope and expectancy. Look at what you have learned so far. Use the skills that you are learning now to change your life. Be a new mom with excellent money-management skills, who can stretch a dollar further than she ever thought could. Begin to teach your children about money as they grow, so they do not repeat any financial mistakes you have made.

For further information on how to become free of financial struggles, www.thelifeofasinglemom.com.

SURVIVING FINANCIAL CRISIS
WEEK 8

Write down what you understand about the principle of tithing. Is this a new concept for you?

_____

_____

_____

_____

What does 2 Corinthians 9:7–8 say about giving?

_____

_____

_____

_____

Take time right now to list every bill you owe. Include all debts and monthly utilities. You must keep track of every penny entering and leaving your home.

_____

_____

_____

_____

_____

_____

_____

_____

_____

_____

In reviewing your budget, what areas can you cut back in? Have you been guilty of over-spending? Commit today to live on a very tight budget during this transitional time. Pray for God to help you.

_____

_____

_____

_____

Look at your budget again. What is the smallest debt you owe? Begin to work towards paying it off. What plan do you have to do that?

_____

_____

_____

_____

PRAYER:

Lord, I commit my finances to you. I will be faithful to tithe ten percent of my income to you. I am committed to changing my spending habits and being a good steward of all you have given me. Amen.

SURVIVING FINANCIAL CRISIS
WEEK 9

What are three areas in which a Credit Bureau Report is used in your life?

_____

_____

_____

_____

Write Psalm 37:20 here. What does this teach you about your debts?

_____

_____

_____

_____

What are three potential reasons for unsatisfactory credit ratings?

_____

_____

_____

_____

Order a copy of your credit report online through Transunion, Experian, and Equifax. In the meantime, begin making a list of any creditors that you know you owe and their phone numbers. Begin to contact them this week about paying those debts.

_____

_____

_____

_____

_____

_____

_____

_____

Explore the world of coupons and discounts. Over the next thirty days, list one magazine, newspaper, or internet source per week that you find useful in helping to save your family money.

_____

_____

_____

_____

When you think of your current financial situation, list the emotions that come to mind.

_____

_____

_____

_____

PRAYER:

God, I am determined to positively impact my financial situation. Help me to remain faithful in paying off all the debts I owe. Keep me motivated to take action with my finances. I pray that I will not become overwhelmed or discouraged. Amen.

CHAPTER 12

HERE WE GO 'ROUND THE MULBERRY BUSH—CYCLES

Stop and think about your life for a moment. Think about how you grew up. Are there things that happened to you as a child that still affect you today? Have you repeated some of the mistakes that your parents made? Have you repeated the same mistake more than once?

We all have had a friend (or been the one) that drinks too much, parties too hard, or moves from one meaningless relationship to another. She may use drugs or watch pornography. She always seems to be the life of the party. She may even experience periods of time when she is genuinely happy with her life. Then, she crashes. She hates life, hates men, and hates herself. And she swears to never drink, smoke, do drugs, or party ever again.

It usually isn't long before she is back at it again. Do you ever wonder why she cannot stop? Are you the girl that cannot stop, and you are frustrated and wonder why?

Any time you have a great night at the bar or dance club, drinking and partying, it always ends. Always. When you wake up the next morning (usually with a great deal of regret about what you did the night before), all you have to show for it is a hangover and some momentary happiness. Many people spend their lives on this emotional roller coaster. Everything is great. It is wonderful. Then, in the next moment, life is terrible. Bobby hates me. I need a drink.

The fact that you are a single mom already opens you up to many unfavorable statistics. Single moms are more likely to have children who become single parents. According to a University of Chicago study sited by CNN in November, 1999, seventy-eight percent of the prison population were raised by single parents. That same study states that the children of inmates are twenty times more likely to go to prison themselves. Cycles.

Alcoholics produce alcoholics. My dad was an alcoholic who loved to hang out in the bars all night. My mother was killed by an alcoholic. Ironically, I found myself, only a few short years later, drinking too much. My father was verbally abusive to me as I grew up. When I had my own children, I began that same pattern of using profanity and screaming at my children early on in their lives. More cycles.

I have counseled women that are on government assistance, who represent four generations of families on government assistance. I have worked with many young girls who gave birth at thirteen or fourteen years old, only to find out that their mothers and grandmothers were also teen moms. I have personally witnessed dozens of cases of generational abuse. The grandmother beat the mother. Now, the mother beats her daughter, and so on. Cycles! Cycles! Cycles!

We never plan to get caught in the middle of bondage, bad lifestyle choices, and vicious cycles of abuse. A woman never plans to become a prostitute. It wasn't her lifetime dream. A drug addict did not believe that her first puff of marijuana would lead to addiction. As a mom, you never plan to abuse your children. A young girl who grew up watching her mother get beaten over and over again by her boyfriend vows to never be the victim of such a crime. Yet, all of these things happen frequently.

And, they happen slowly, often without us noticing.

Verbal, emotional, physical, and sexual abuse is commonly repeated through generations. Alcoholism, grief, depression, single parenting, poverty, and sexual promiscuity can also lend itself to generational cycles. Cycles destroy our future. They destroy our hope for tomorrow. They limit us from seeing where we can go because we only see where we came from, what Momma was, what Daddy was.

Sexual sin is one of the strongest bondages affecting us today. The subject is often avoided. Many churches avoid talking about it for fear that they will alienate their congregations. Parents do not talk to their children about it. Yet, it is the raging beast that so closely binds many of the other cycles; alcoholism, single parenting, financial destruction, depression, etc.

1 Corinthians 6:18–20 says, "Run from sexual sin! No other sin as clearly affects the body as this one does. For sexual immorality is a sin against your own body. Don't you realize that your body is a temple of the Holy Spirit, who lives in you and was given to you by God? You do not belong to yourself for God bought you with a high price. So you must honor God with your body."

Here are some statistics directly related to sexual immorality:

- 22% of all pregnancies end in abortion (Stomacher Institute, July 2008).

- From 1978–2008, more than 45 million babies have been aborted (Guttmacher Institute, July 2008).

- Almost 37,000 people per year are diagnosed with AIDS (reported by State Health Departments, 2008).

- More than 70% of men between eighteen to thirty-four years old have viewed pornography (SafeFamilies.org).

- Sixty-seven percent of divorce is directly related to infidelity (MenStuff.org).

- The average age a woman gets into prostitution is age fourteen. She stays in it an average of eleven years. Eighty-two percent of all prostitutes were raped (U.S. Department of Justice, 2007).

Movies and television glamorize sexual immorality to make it appealing to the viewer.

Anything goes. Do what feels right. Read the statistics above again. Does this feel right? The facts above are staggering, but they do not address the even bigger problems. They do not talk about the depression, loneliness, insecurity, and trauma that the individuals are left with after poor choices. In spite of the emotional damage, in spite of God's word, and in spite of the statistics that vehemently support avoiding sex outside of marriage, we still continue to pursue this bondage.

So, how do we stop this? How do we stop running to the very things that have made us, our parents, and many before them miserable? You must first recognize what is going on. Recognize that you are in the midst of a cycle. That is the hardest part. Many times we see our parents get abused or be the abuser. We see them become alcoholics, so we secretly think that is going to be us in twenty years. Even statistics support it. Why is that? It is very simple. We condition ourselves to expect less. We begin to see ourselves just like our parents were. Although we are told over and over as children that we can do anything or be anything, we simply do not believe it. In fact, I would venture to say that some of our parents did not believe it. In my years of counseling, I have seen the mother of a young child say, "Brian that is wonderful. Of course, you can be an astronaut! You can do anything!" But once life has taken a toll and she has had hardships of her own, I have seen that same mother say to her son, now slightly older, "Brian, sit down and shut up. You are not going to be anything but a loser just like your loser father was!"

As mothers, we must be extremely cautious of what we speak over our children. Your child's future depends on it. Your child can be anything. She can do anything.

And guess what? You can, too. Stop believing that you will always live on government assistance. Do not accept less than God's best for your life. Begin to see yourself as a daughter of the King of Kings. Demand better for yourself.

I was driving across town the other day and began to turn the dial of the radio to different talk shows. I finally landed on a financial advice talk show, although I am not sure who it was. He made a comment that I found interesting. Studies have shown that most people are only as wealthy as the average of their five closest friends. Isn't that amazing? Since you have decided (consciously or subconsciously) that you will never make more money than your parents did or that your friends do, then you won't.

You have already seen three generations in your family become alcoholics, so I guess that means you are going to fall into that pit also. Your grandmother and your mother were single moms. You are a single mom. Doesn't that mean that your daughter is doomed to more of the same? No.

Consider Emily. I worked with Emily for over a year. She came to me two months pregnant. She had been a drug addict for over ten years. She was raised in a violent home by a mother who was addicted to drugs. Her mother began to give her drugs at a young age. Although I have seen drug addicts and abuse victims many times, there was something about Emily that just drew me to her. She seemed like an innocent young girl who just needed to be loved.

We began to invest time and resources into her. She went through a drug rehabilitation program. She began to go to church two or three times a week. We monitored her visitors closely. We threw her a surprise baby shower. She developed close friends through the church. After the birth of her baby, she enrolled in college and began to look for a job. She seemed to be going on the right track.

Within weeks, she had reconnected with her old boyfriend. She began to smoke and drink the first night she was with him. The drugs quickly followed. Before I knew what was happening, I lost complete contact with Emily and later learned that she was back in drug rehabilitation only a few months later.

Nikki was a twenty-year-old college student who came to me at six months pregnant. She had completed thirteen drug rehabilitation programs. She too seemed to be a sweet, innocent girl who had been caught up with the wrong crowd. She had moved from several states away. She had separated from the wrong influences in her life. She went through the pregnancy drug-free. She began to attend church and had plans to complete college and work in the medical field. Nikki gave birth to a healthy baby girl. Within forty-eight hours, she was released from the hospital and went home with her newborn. She asked her father if she could borrow his car to make a run to the grocery store for diapers. She disappeared. We later learned that she had connected with a new boyfriend and was high on drugs again. Her mother eventually took that baby to raise.

Emily and Nikki broke my heart. With each woman that comes through my door, I believe the best for her. I truly believe that she can change her life. I believe that her past is now behind her and begin to look toward her future. So, why did they both go back to drugs? The problem was that they did not believe their lives could be different. They were both raised in drug-infested homes with lackluster parents. No matter what they said to me, inside, they believed that they would go back to their old lifestyles eventually. As much as I loved those two girls, I cannot believe hard enough for them. They have to believe they can change. They must see themselves as new in Christ.

Casey was different. Casey came from a similar background as Nikki and Emily. She used drugs, became an unwed mother, and lived in her car. She came to me tired and scared with few friends, on the verge of financial ruin. She, too, dedicated her life to the Lord and became committed to attending church and Bible studies. There was something in her eyes that made me know that she was serious. She began slowly to speak up during Bible groups. She volunteered with the local church. She began to ask new friends out for coffee. Now, more than a year later, she is financially flourishing, drug free, sexually pure, and employed with an outreach that serves other single mothers. Her story is one of the many successful stories that keep me motivated to continue the journey.

What makes her story different from the two others? Casey truly believed she could do it. She believed that Christ's power in her life was sufficient to cover all past hurt and mistakes.

The great news is that the Bible says that is available for anyone. We do not have to be bound by our parents' choices. In fact, we do not have to be bound by our own poor choices from the past.

Second Corinthians 5:17 says, "This means that anyone who belongs to Christ has become a new person. The old life is gone; a new life has begun!" This means you have the freedom to make new decisions. You no longer live in the bondage of who you were before you became a Christian. That's exciting news, right? You decide what the outcome of your life will be on how you choose to live. Choose life.

CYCLES
WEEK 10

Is there a situation from your childhood that you have since repeated in your adult life, such as alcoholism, abuse, screaming at your children, financial irresponsibility, or sexual promiscuity?

_____

_____

_____

_____

Sexual sin can devastate us both emotionally and physically. List a few ways here.

_____

_____

_____

_____

What does 1 Corinthians 6:18–20 say about sexual sin?

_____

_____

_____

_____

Has there been a time in your life when you have spoken negativity over your children? Have you said things that you did not mean? Have you been a poor example to them? Take the time to ask forgiveness from your Heavenly Father and your children now.

_____

_____

_____

_____

Read 2 Corinthians 5:17. Do you believe that you are a new person in Christ?

_____

_____

_____

_____

PRAYER:

Lord, help me break the cycles that have held me captive in my family. I refuse to repeat another poor choice. I ask for your guidance with my choices.

CHAPTER 13

WHOM THE SON SETS FREE ...

As we come to the end of our journey together, I pray you have learned a great deal about yourself. We have covered everything from finances to parenting with many roads bridged in between. It is only fitting that I end the book with freedom. As you embark on this new life of parenting alone (and have just learned some new skills to do it), it is important that you feel empowered to move on. You need the confidence to persevere. Freedom offers you such confidence.

Freedom in Christ is the tie that binds every area we have talked about. We must be free to parent effectively, free to manage our finances appropriately, and free to relinquish emotional fears and doubts.

This country affords us such things as Freedom of Speech and Freedom of Religion. Thank God for those things. Thank God that we can go to church on Sundays. We can open our Bibles as we wish. We are free to worship in the streets, if we choose. All those things represent freedom. But what is true freedom?

There is one of two places where you live your life: freedom or bondage. There is not a halfway point. You do not straddle the fence with one leg in freedom and the other in bondage. Many words or phrases come to mind as I think about freedom and its opposite, bondage. This should give you a clearer picture of one's emotional state with each list.

BONDAGE	FREEDOM
Suffocation	Joy
Shackled	Peace
Confusion	Happiness
Fear	Fearless
Anxiety	Uninhibited
Hindered	Running & Skipping
Ashamed	Sun on my face
Embarrassed	Wrapped in a warm blanket
Addicted	Forgiveness
Slavery	Guilt-Free
Bitterness	Wings
Chains	Wind blowing through my hair

As you read through each list, is there one that you most closely identify with? Which list would you prefer to identify with?

In order for you to adequately understand freedom, it is crucial for you to understand bondage. Through the years, I have discussed Christianity with many people. I have had comments, such as, "That Christian thing is just too restrictive. I cannot live my life that way," or "I will live my life for Jesus in a few years, when I am older and settle down. Just let me find a husband, first." I remember thinking many of the same things in my life. For years, I thought that God just did not want us to have any fun. I have since come to a deeper understanding of what God wants for us.

Think of it in this way. As a mother, you love your children more than words can express. You have watched them grow from infants, to toddlers, and into adolescence. As they grow, there are times we must say no. For example, Johnny wants to climb onto a cabinet to reach the cookie jar. Sarah wants to go driving with her friend Susie, who has already been in two wrecks this year. Jonathan wants to go to a party where there will be no adult supervision. Your child's immediate response very well could be, "Mom never wants me to have any fun. She just wants to control me and make my life miserable."

God is our heavenly Father who created us. He loves us. He desires for us to live lives full of happiness, joy, and fun. In order to do that, there are things that he must also disapprove of. Rather than looking at things as restrictions, I challenge you to look at them as hot burners on a stove that you do not want to touch. If ignored, they can hurt you and leave permanent scars.

Why are we to stay away from drugs and alcohol? They lead to a path of destruction in our bodies. Have you ever seen someone addicted to drugs, whether on television or in person? We have been given one body to care for to the best of our abilities. Feeding our body poison would not be the best way to take care of it. God already knows that for whatever temporary enjoyment drugs and alcohol could offer, there is a lifetime of pain associated with it.

Pornography offers the same type of bondage. As you watch one smutty movie or glimpse at one inappropriate picture, you may wonder, "What's the harm?" Pornography has destroyed many marriages. It distorts our view of what should be meant as wholesome and pure. Once we have viewed such things, it is almost impossible to remove the images from our mind. One glimpse usually leads to two or three, then daily, then hours on end. It is an addiction of the worst kind, as most people are too ashamed or embarrassed to admit to the addiction. There is such shame attached to it. As with most addictions, the addict only admits there is a problem after their whole world is destroyed—loss of spouse, job, family, and money.

Sexual immorality is another big one that I hear arguments supporting. "Well, I love my boyfriend and it is not like I am with anyone else. I am faithful to him." "I have needs." "I am lonely. I do not want to be alone. He will not stay with me unless I do." "I just want to have some fun. I have earned that right. I have been a good girl all my life." There are hundreds, if not thousands, of statistics that support reasons to avoid sexual immorality, STDs, AIDS, and unplanned pregnancies. How fun is it when that man that you have physically given yourself to decides that he is no longer interested or he becomes unfaithful? Any loneliness you felt prior to a sexual encounter will not be cured with it. In fact, the likelihood of having a more severe bout of loneliness after he leaves you is almost inevitable.

Lastly, think about lying and deceit. When you begin entangling yourself and others in a web of lies, there is no end in sight. We all know the drill. You tell a little white lie to avoid an uncomfortable situation. Then, you must lie again to cover up that lie. Before you know what has happened, you are immersed in a sea of lies of which you cannot remember the truth. It leads to an internal war. It leads to an uncomfortable feeling in the pit of your stomach.

Every area above leads to emotional torment and bondage. Our Father in heaven does not want that for us. He wants us to enjoy our lives. The emotional consequences of choosing to live a life outside of God's will leave us in a state of confusion, unrest, and unhappiness.

Consider the following verses:

I will walk in freedom, for I have devoted myself to your commandments (Psalm 119:45).

For you have been called to live in freedom, my brothers and sisters. But don't use your freedom to satisfy your sinful nature. Instead, use your freedom to serve one another in love (Galatians 5:13).

And you will know the truth, and the truth will set you free.
But we are descendants of Abraham, they said. We have never been slaves to anyone.
What do you mean, 'You will be set free?' Jesus replied, I tell you the truth, everyone who sins is a slave of sin. A slave is not a permanent member of the family,

but a son is a part of the family forever. So if the Son
sets you free, you are truly free (John 8:32–36).

I want to jump out of my seat when I hear this! It cannot be more plain. The Bible explains to us that there is
no freedom in living a life of sin. We wind up deeper and
deeper in misery. Because God designed us, he knows the
intricacies of our spirit, our emotions, and our physical
wellbeing. We must trust that he has our best interest at
heart, just as you love your children and have their best
interests in mind. Freedom comes from knowing you are
fine not to accept that invitation to become involved with
drugs, alcohol, pornography, sexual immorality, or deceit.

When I think of living a life in total freedom, I think
of peace. Peace in the world means there is no active con-
flict, no war going on around you. There can be complete
peace all around you, yet a war rages internally. You are
haunted by a past hurt or offense. You are living with a past
sin that you cannot forgive yourself of. You want to choose
the right thing, but you keep doing the wrong things, it
seems. God's peace is confidence in any circumstance.

The secret to God's peace is to appreciate His perfect
timing. Let's see what the Bible says about timing:

For everything there is a season, a time for every activity under the sun. A time to be born and a time to die.
A time to plant and a time to harvest. A time to kill
and a time to heal. A time to tear down and a time to
build up. A time to cry and a time to laugh. A time to
grieve and a time to dance. A time to scatter stones and
a time to gather stones. A time to embrace and a time
to throw away. A time to tear and a time to mend. A

time to be quiet and a time to speak. A time to love and a time to hate. A time for war and a time for peace.

Ecclesiastes 3:1–8

Some of you need permission right now to move into a new season. I am telling you that for some of you, that new season is here. There is a time to cry and a time to mourn, but you will notice that those are followed by times of laughing, dancing, and mending. Understand that being at peace with God's timing does not mean that you love every minute of it. It does not mean that you enjoy the learning process you are in. It simply means that you are at peace to accept that God is in control, that He will take care of it, and you will be just fine.

When you go through deep waters, I will be with you. When you go through rivers of difficulty, you will not drown. When you walk through the fire of oppression, you will not be burned up; the flames will not consume you.

Isaiah 43:2

That is a comforting word . Some of you find peace in knowing God is with you to help you through your trials, but for others of you, you cannot accept this peace. You cannot accept God's love. You are bound up with the thought of, "But you do not know what I have done in my past." This is when you discover that we all have different areas that we must gain freedom. You need to walk through forgiveness. What are some different areas of forgiveness available to you?

FREEDOM TO GIVE AND RECEIVE FORGIVENESS

As Christians, we talk about how God forgives us of our sin. We talk about how much God loves us and how wonderful his grace and mercy are. But if you do not understand the depth of His love and mercy, you can still struggle with the concept of not being good enough. For some, your past has tormented you. It is eating you alive, gnawing at you day and night. Some of you are disgusted by things you have done, things you have seen, or heard. I have good news for you.

> Can anything ever separate us from Christ's love? Does it mean he no longer loves us if we have trouble or calamity, or are persecuted, or hungry, or destitute, or in danger or threatened with death? No, despite all these things, overwhelming victory is ours through Christ, who loved us.
>
> Romans 8:35, 37

Your guilt has overwhelmed you. You have lived in embarrassment and shame. But God is saying to you today, his victory overwhelms us. Do not dwell on what you have done wrong. Ask forgiveness from your heavenly Father and to those whom you have offended (whether they accept it or not) and move on. Accept his forgiveness.

The flip side of receiving forgiveness is giving forgiveness. Giving forgiveness is for your benefit. You are not granting forgiveness for the benefit of the other person. The inability to forgive in itself is bitterness. You are granting forgiveness so that you can move past the offense. I have seen many, many people allow un-forgiveness to age them beyond their years. Bitterness causes not only the physical appearance to change, but the emotional wellbeing to shrivel.

Let me release you of a potential fear you may have. Forgiveness does not mean acceptance of the offense and it does not mean trust. You are not saying that what you have endured is okay. You may have been raped or molested. Maybe you were beaten or abused. Perhaps you had a spouse that was unfaithful or suffered with an addiction, such as alcohol or pornography. You may be raising your child alone because his father abandoned you. None of those things are acceptable behaviors. Your forgiveness merely means that this event no longer dictates the rest of your life. You are a whole person in Christ and can honestly forgive the offender.

Do not wait on someone to ask for forgiveness. Forgive others before you are asked. Truthfully, you may never receive such a request. Your offender could die, be imprisoned, disappear, or simply have a hardened heart. You do not want to die in bitterness and un-forgiveness. What kind of life does that offer you? What will you have gained by harboring un-forgiveness for the rest of your life? Will you have in some way hurt the one who hurt you? No, but what you will have done is lived a life in bondage to that un-forgiveness. We are talking about living a life of freedom.

I challenge you with Luke 23:34. "Jesus said, 'Father, forgive them for they do not know what they are doing.'" Right before Jesus was killed, he asked his father in heaven to forgive those who were putting him to death, the soldiers who spat on him, the Jewish leaders, the Roman politicians, and bystanders. Jesus is our ultimate example of forgiveness. As he hung on a cross, drowning in his own blood, dying a slow death, guilty of nothing, he forgave those who had hurt him. He did not wait for them to ask for his forgiveness.

FREEDOM TO ACCEPT DISCIPLINE

Accepting discipline can be a bitter pill to swallow if our hearts are not right. Just as it is necessary for you to discipline your children appropriately, it is also necessary for our heavenly Father to give such discipline. This gives us further evidence of his love for us.

Proverbs 3:11–12 says, "My child, don't reject the Lord's discipline, and don't be upset when he corrects you. For the Lord corrects those he loves, just as a father corrects a child in who he delights." When we ignore discipline, we back ourselves into a corner that is hard to get out of.

I can look back in my own life and see these truths so evidently. As I mentioned earlier, I have attended church most of my life. I have been taught biblical principles from early childhood. I understood that children are to obey their parents and that sex before marriages is wrong. Yet, I chose to move in the wrong direction in both those areas. When I was caught as an early teenager disobeying my dad's instructions and pursuing an unhealthy relationship, I did not ask for forgiveness. I secretly plotted on how I would be more aloof the next time. My thought was, *How can I not get caught again?* Not *What can I learn from this mistake?*

My first sexual encounter did not lead to pregnancy, but it was my inability to accept discipline and learn from my mistakes that ultimately did. Because I was unwilling to accept appropriate teaching and discipline by both my earthly and heavenly fathers, I have since walked out the consequences of mistakes made twenty years ago.

Oftentimes, we are overflowing with pride and arrogance, and simply do not want to admit to a mistake. We fail to accept discipline, because we will not admit there was ever a wrong-doing. We gloss over it. We pretend it never happened.

Proverbs 19:3 says, "People ruin their lives by their own foolishness and then are angry at the Lord."

Imagine how your life would be if you were free to accept discipline from your heavenly Father, your earthly parents, your boss, or even a mentor. When we have a receptive spirit and are open to receiving correction, we grow. Parenting our own children has much more to do with our heart towards God and our ability to receive correction, for how can we give correction and not receive it?

FREEDOM OVER ADDICTION

1 Corinthians 10:13 says, The temptations in your life are no different from what others experience. And God is faithful. He will not allow the temptation to be more than you can stand. When you are tempted, he will show you a way out so you can endure.

Praise God! He is saying that he will never give us something we cannot handle with his help. We have already discussed the destructive lifestyle that addiction can bring about. There are times when the pressures of the world may come down on you so heavy that it feels like you cannot take it another second, but take heart. God's word is true and he is promising you that when you are tempted, there will be a way out.

One thing that I have seen surface repeatedly when dealing with addiction is manipulation. The addict manipulates others into believing he wants to get better. He manipulates situations and circumstances so that he can feed his addiction in private. In fact, I have found that as time passes, addicts do not even realize they are manipulating friends and family. He can even manipulate the church into believing that he wants a new life. Be aware of this. Ask forgiveness from God and others if you have used manipulation to feed your addiction.

As an addict, you may not recognize if you are being manipulative. Begin to ask yourself some key questions. "Do I really believe what I just said, or do I simply want to be right?" "Do I have the desire to always be in control of every situation?" "Is this an issue that needs discussing, or am I turning this into an argument to avoid the real issue?" "Am I willing and ready to change my current lifestyle, or am I saying I want to change to buy more time?"

Once you have made up your mind that you are tired of the lifestyle, the destruction that your addiction causes, then you begin the process of achieving freedom over it. Seek help immediately. Do not wait a few days or few weeks to see how you do on your own. The longer you wait, the easier it is to fall back into the addiction trap. Call your local church. Counselors are usually available and equipped with useful recovery information for addicts that range from substance abuse to pornography and beyond. Many cities have free group therapy and even have licensed therapists available at discount rates.

Let's not pretend that it is an easy journey, for we all know it is not. But the end result is a lifetime of happiness and freedom that no pill or drink could ever give.

FREEDOM TO NOT BE RIGHT

If I had to choose one area that has been an on-going struggle with me (not that there have not been many), this would be it. I have strong convictions and opinions and desire to have everyone agree. I believe there may be one or two of you out there that suffer in this area as well, so I offer you my thoughts.

I have spoken to you throughout the book about the job I landed after I began tithing back in my early twenties. I spent almost ten years with the company. I know that the Lord orchestrated me being there, and it was by his grace that I obtained such an immeasurable blessing. I will be forever grateful for all the things I learned there. My success with the company allowed my confidence to soar. My presentation and public speaking skills skyrocketed. My income increased dramatically. All of those were direct results of training from that company.

However, with increased confidence came increased arrogance and a total lack of humility. This was a gradual process. I won an award or received a promotion. I was called upon to speak to my colleagues during a presentation. Before I knew it, I had become extremely arrogant. I knew that I was good at my job and could not take direction well. If I was approached by a superior about changing a procedure, I became defensive. I argued with colleagues, supervisors, and other departments. I was always right. When it came to my management style, it was similar. I ruled with an iron fist. Employees dare not question my directives, or they would be sorry! My intention was never to become difficult. It happened because it was more important for me to be right than to maintain relationships.

I had a conversation with my beloved aunt one day. My aunt has been a Christian all her life and has been married to the same man for over fifty years. She has been a mentor, prayer warrior, and close friend for many years. I do not remember what started the conversation or what else we spoke about, but I did retain one key sentence. She said, "In the many years that I have been a Christian and maintained a marriage, I have learned one thing. It is more important to maintain the relationship than it is to be right. You give up your right to be right when you forge relationships."

She never knew how deeply that affected me. I was married to a caring, loving man, who was God's gift to me, and I never conceded an argument. I was always right in marriage, parenting, and business. Even now, I can remember how off-putting that was for others. I have since learned that the words of wisdom my aunt offered that day were far more valuable than any gift she could have given me. I treasure them even now.

There is nothing wrong with having strong convictions. There are injustices that should anger us. Our reaction to these convictions and anger is where the freedom comes in. I have now learned that every wrong in the world does not have to be righted by me. I do not need a cause to fight for, just for the sake of fighting for a cause. Every conversation does not need to end in an argument or a submission that I am the queen of knowledge on every subject. And I am okay with that. Whew! What freedom!

FREEDOM TO TRUST IN THE LORD

Do you remember falling in the love for the very first time? Maybe it was a high school sweetheart or a college classmate. Do you remember how you wanted to spend every waking moment getting to know him? You wanted to know about their family, their beliefs, as much as you possibly could. Let me challenge you with a different question. What about your heavenly Father? Do you want to spend time with him getting to know who he is and what he's like?

Many claim to believe in God or even love him. Yet, they never step foot inside a church, read their Bible, seek his will for their lives, or pray. Would that same approach to a new relationship work in your dating life? God knew you before you were even born. He knew you would make mistakes and he chose to send his son anyway. We all come from different religious backgrounds. Even among Christians, there are differences of opinion and different denominations. However, as I have said many times before, being a Christian is not about religion or some rituals that you perform every Sunday. It is about a relationship. God gives us freedom from religion in order to experience true relationship.

Relationships take time to develop. You must get to know one another. You do not end a relationship with a boyfriend, husband, or even a family member because something does not go your way. Then why is it that so many give their lives over to God (half-heartedly), and when He does not answer their prayers immediately in the way they see fit, they decide that this God-thing is not for them?

> When Pharaoh finally let the people go; God did not lead them along the main road that runs through Philistine territory, even though that was the shortest distance to the Promised Land. God said, 'If the people are faced with a battle, they might change their minds and return to Egypt.' So God led them in a roundabout way through the wilderness toward the Red Sea. Thus the Israelites left Egypt like an army ready for battle.
>
> Exodus 13:17–18

To give you a brief background, the Israelites were slaves to the Egyptians and had been severely mistreated through many years of bondage. God chose Moses to deliver the Israelites to freedom. Pharaoh would not let the Israelites leave willingly, so God sent a series of plagues to Egypt that tormented the Egyptians. Pharaoh finally relented. This is where the scripture above picks up. After having been beaten and abused for many years, one would think that the last thing on the Israelites mind would be to turn around and go back. However, as we see above, God knew that they would want to go back if they encountered trouble. Isn't that true of us all? When the going gets tough, we sometimes want to tuck our tails and run rather than see what wonderful thing is in store for us on the other side. Sometimes, even if there is something better ahead, we want to run back to what we know, what is comfortable. The key to freedom is pressing past this point.

Trusting in the Lord does not mean we have it all figured out. In fact, quite the opposite is true. The freedom comes in accepting that you will never have it all figured out, even if you spent the rest of your life in church every Sunday and attended Bible college the other days of the week.

> My thoughts are nothing like your thoughts," says the Lord. "And my ways are far beyond anything you could imagine. For just as the heavens are higher than the earth, so my ways are higher than your ways and my thoughts higher than your thoughts.
>
> Isaiah 55:8–9

This is one of the best ways to explain it. God has it all figured out and our job is to obey, not question, him.

There have been times in my life when I was wrapped up in a number of the bondages we have discussed. The problem was that I did not realize it. I could not figure out why I did not seem to have the true joy that Christians talk about, that the Bible talks about. The joy comes in making the Lord your personal King of kings, Lord of lords, and ruler of your heart. If anything else rules your thoughts, such as bitterness, un-forgiveness, addictions, and deceit, then he cannot rule there.

As I have moved into the most recent season of my own life, I rest in the true freedom that is a relationship with Christ. I do not have to always be right` or have things figured out. I do not need to overanalyze the next step. I trust in the Lord. As different areas of my own life need improving, so will yours. I may grab onto bitterness and not let it go. Then, after recognizing it and working through it, I release it. But inevitably, something else creeps up, perhaps anger, or a harsh tongue, but something. We are not perfect. We never will be.

Accept right now that you will never be the absolute perfect mom. Recognize that you will not always say the right things. You will never have the perfect face or perfect body shape, according to what the world's standard portrays. But most importantly, recognize that you are the perfect one to raise your child. God chose you. Recognize that you have the perfect appearance, made just for you, courtesy of your gracious and loving heavenly Father. Accept his mercy and grace. Work hard to be the best you can be in all areas and allow yourself to be forgiven when you fail.

The prayer that I wrote in my journal many years ago and refer to often is as follows.

Search me, Father. Reveal areas in my life that I am not right in. Forgive me. Help me know that every single day is a fresh start. My beginning starts today, right now. It is new. Lord, thank you that your grace is sufficient and that your mercy is new every morning. Give me an excitement for my life. Remind me daily what my purpose is. Give me the grace to walk in that purpose and allow me to forgive myself, just as you have forgiven me. Amen.

Imagine what type of mom you would be if you allowed God to fight your battles. We get caught up in wanting to be right, seeking revenge on those who hurt us, or feeling sorry for what has been done to us. We do not give it to God. I challenge you today to turn it all over to him. Begin to see yourself as a new person, a new creation. Start your life, today. Look at parenting with a new perspective. Respect what God has given you. The Creator of this world has entrusted you with the life of a son or daughter. Be honored. Be free.

WHOM THE SON SETS FREE...
WEEK 11

Describe freedom in your own words.

_____

_____

_____

_____

What is bondage? What are some areas in which you have experienced bondage?

_____

_____

_____

_____

As Christians, we choose to walk in freedom by avoiding sin. It holds us captive. What does Psalm 119:45 say about this?

_____

_____

_____

_____

Consider forgiveness. Is there someone in your life that you need to forgive? Are you withholding forgiveness from yourself in any area? Let go of it today. Decide today that bitterness, un-forgiveness, and shame will not hold you captive.

_____

_____

_____

_____

Has there been a time in your life when it was difficult to accept discipline? How do you think this affects your ability to discipline your children?

_____

_____

_____

_____

Write Proverbs 3:11–12 here.

_____

_____

_____

PRAYER:

Heavenly Father, there are many areas where I have lived in bondage. I have walked through life feeling burdened by my past. Release me of that right now. Allow me to release myself of it. Allow me to be free to accept and give forgiveness. Allow me to accept and give discipline in an appropriate manner. Amen.

WHOM THE SON SETS FREE...
WEEK 12

Do you struggle with the need to always be right? Is it important to you to have others share your opinion? Ask God to reveal to you those areas where you should stand your ground and those where you should resolve to keep quiet.

_____

_____

_____

_____

Do you give every area of your life to the Lord? Do you trust him with your finances, your relationships, and your parenting?

_____

_____

_____

_____

Release yourself right now from any need to be perfect. Allow yourself room to make mistakes and grow. Write a promise to yourself here.

_____

_____

_____

_____

Take the time right now to write a prayer to God. Bear your heart and soul to him on paper.

_____

_____

_____

_____

_____

_____

_____

_____

Make a list of areas in your life in which you are thankful. Refer to it often.

_____

_____

_____

_____

_____

_____

_____

_____

PRAYER:

Thank you, Lord, that I am changed. Thank you for all you have revealed to me through this book and your Word. Continue to change me and grow me. Help me not be who I was. I praise you for your grace and mercy. Amen.

PART THREE

LEADER'S GUIDES

LEADER'S GUIDE

Years ago, when I started my first Single Mom's Support Group, I struggled to find resources to help me along the way. I was super-excited to connect with single moms and offer them encouragement and friendship. I wanted to steward their time well by offering some Godly wisdom, but also have lots of laughs and develop great friendships. I had no idea in those early days that my first support group would lead to the development of a global organization, The Life of a Single Mom Ministries (TLSM). At the time of this book's writing, TLSM has launched more than 1,500 single mother's support groups globally. Only God could do such a thing!

My hope in providing this Leader's Guide is to continue to encourage successful single mother's support groups. We want to see single mothers around the world connecting to churches that have these support groups. Our hope at TLSM is to see all single mothers connected in a church support group for single moms, where they can feel challenged, encouraged, and safe. This Leader's Guide was written with the intention giving you Best Practices for Single Mom's Support Groups. You will find that each week of the Bible study has questions and a suggested prayer. This guide will offer tips for fostering great discussion.

The most important piece of the single mom support group puzzle is relationships, relationships, relationships! It is approximated that almost 70 percent of single mothers in the United States are not actively attending a local church in their community. There are many reasons for this. The last thing an unchurched or newly churched single mother needs to hear is a list of thirteen things that she is doing wrong! It can be perceived as judgment and it is just the thing the enemy would use to keep her from coming back. That said, the most important thing you can do as a Support Group Leader is to develop relationships. Get to know the moms. Understand who they are, how they think, where they work, their hopes and dreams for their kiddos. This will later open the door for ministry to take place. It is almost impossible to minister Godly advice into her life, until you have fostered that strong relationship with her first.

The next things you will want to consider when conducting a Single Mom's Support Group are childcare and meal provision. Having a single mom's Bible study or support group without offering childcare is like having a peanut butter sandwich without the jelly. You can't have one without the other. The same is true for a meal. Whether you are hosting a small group with three to four single mothers or a larger group with several hundred, having a meal at the Bible study removes one more obstacle that may keep the mother away from the group. Both free meals and childcare can be provided without costing you, the facilitator, or the church (if applicable) any money. Simply put together a volunteer database of those in your community who would like to serve single mothers. Simply put volunteers on a rotating schedule for cooking meals and/or babysitting.

Leaders, also consider the length of your meetings. All

of us have been part of a Bible study that droned on far too long or had a Sister Talks-A-Lot who made the meeting far too lengthy. Single moms are busy, as are all moms. We have found that those Bible studies who are intentional with their time and start and end on time are the ones that are most frequently attended and consistently grow. That's not to say that you cannot have a time of fellowship after the meeting for those moms who want to stay and chat. But formally ending the meeting with an announcement that the group is now over gives those moms who do need to rush home and iron or wash clothes or finish homework the time to do so.

The other thing I would mention about the Bible study in this book is to go at your own pace. I developed the Bible study with the intention of spending extra time on those areas that may need some extra TLC. For example, there are two separate parts to the Overcoming Abuse chapter. This could be taught over the course of two meetings. But when I taught these to some local single moms here in Louisiana, I stayed on that chapter for 4 meetings. In other words, embrace flexibility. There may be a meeting where the Holy Spirit is really ministering to women and you only get through one question of the curriculum. Use discernment to simply move on the following week or camp out there several weeks.

Above all else, have fun! Create an environment where single moms can come be part of a relaxed, fun, atmosphere where there are giggles and surprises and putting your feet up on the furniture is allowed! They deserve it.

For tons of other great tips and resources for hosting successful single moms' event, Bible studies, and outreaches, visit www.thelifeofasinglemom.com.

Overwhelmed Leaders Guide
Introduction to the Curriculum

Food and Fellowship: (Suggested time: 30 minutes)

This time can be used for meal distribution, games, ice breakers, introduction, and opening prayer, taking care to make any new attendees feel welcome and having some fun. (Note: This can also include live worship or pre-recorded music).

- **Opening Prayer**
- **Welcome & Introductions**
- **Ice Breaker:** What's the best piece of advice you've ever been given? When you die, what do you want to be remembered for? What is your favorite item you've bought this year? (Note: You'll spend a little more time on ice breakers in this lesson, since it's the launch of your new curriculum. Have fun this week! Relationship development will be critical in helping you minister the content.)

Ground Rules: (Note: These are suggestions on ways to help you navigate the curriculum. It's up to you, if you share these or create your own.)

- During discussion time, please limit your responses to 3 or 4 minutes so that others have a chance to participate.
- This class is confidential. What is said in class stays in class. Do not gossip with anyone else in class/outside of class about what's been shared by another.
- To honor your time, we will make every effort to start and end on time.

Lesson Time: (Suggested time: 30 minutes)

Lesson time will include the main points from the assigned reading for each chapter. (Note: Some chapters will be sub-divided into two lessons). Instructors can enhance lesson time by integrating personal stories and testimonials, additional Scripture references, special guest speakers, etc. Since this is week is simply an introduction to curriculum, we suggest you give the attendees an overview of all the lessons that will be covered, as well as prepare some testimonials. This can be you sharing your testimony (if you have a single parenting story), or someone from the church or group. Alternatively, you can have a 5-in-5 testimonial round, where you pre-select 5 ladies to share their testimonies in 5 minutes each. This week is all about relationship development. The more meaningful this meeting, the more likely the ladies will receive the curriculum over the next several weeks.

Content to be covered over the course of the Overwhelmed Curriculum:

- **Overcoming Abuse** – We will spend two meetings discussing the challenges that many have faced in abuses of several kinds, how that has impacted our decision-making, and effective steps to healing from past abuses.
- **Being a Single Parent** – This lesson will cover understanding the challenges that every single parent will face and ways to overcome those challenges.
- **Playing the Victim Role** – Many single mothers have faced trauma, past abuse, emotional scars, and have been victims to many things. This two-part lesson will focus on how to move from victim to victor with effective principles and strategies for success.
- **Parenting 101** – We'll spend two lessons discussing parenting techniques that will be applicable for single mothers whether you have small children or older children. These focus on parenting principles for single mothers.
- **Surviving Financial Crisis** – We'll spend two lessons discussing the various financial challenges that single

mothers face, regardless of socio-economic status, and best practices for managing your money effectively.

- **Cycles** – We know that what we don't address, we'll often repeat. What's worse is that our children are likely to repeat those same unaddressed mistakes. This lesson will detail the cycles often found in single parent homes and how to eradicate those things in your home!

- **Whom the Son Sets Free** – The final two lessons in our series will detail freedom in Christ and what it means to live a life free from bondage. We'll discuss past burdens that can hold one back and how to develop a lifestyle strategy that is effective in breaking current and future chains, so that you can learn to embrace the joy in your single parenting season, not the burden.

Group Discussion Time: (Suggested time: 30 Minutes)
- Describe your ideal life. When you close your eyes and dream, what does that look like?
- What are the things that will prevent you from achieving that dream?
- What are the things you can do to accomplish your dreams? What do you have control over?

Final Thoughts: (5 minutes)

We cannot change the inevitable. The only thing we can do is play on the one string we have, and that is our attitude. I am convinced that life is 10% what happens to me and 90% of how I react to it. And so, it is with you... we are in charge of our Attitudes." — Charles Swindoll

- **Homework Assignment for next meeting:** Read Chapters 1-7 (if you have not already). We'll discuss the similarities we found in the author's story to our own and then begin discussing part I of Overcoming Abuse. Complete study guide on pgs. 90-91.
- **Closing Prayer**

Ministry Leader Tips:
- Relationship development is critical in single mom's ministry. Spend time getting to know your attendees and volunteers.
- Have fun. Create community and laugh! A lot!
- We recommend structure of 30-30-30. 30 minutes of food & fellowship. 30 minutes of lesson time. 30 minutes of discussion time.
- If you have not already done so, now is the time to consider purchasing a ministry kit from The Life of a Single Mom to assist you with training, group development, growth strategies & advertising, logistics,

and long-term sustainability, among others. All information available at www.thelifeofasinglemom.com.

Overwhelmed Leader's Guide
Meeting 1:
Overcoming Abuse (Part I)

Food and Fellowship: (Suggested time: 30 minutes)

This time can be used for meal distribution, games, ice breakers, introduction, and opening prayer, taking care to make any new attendees feel welcome and having some fun. (Note: This can also include live worship or pre-recorded music).

- **Opening Prayer**

- **Welcome & Introductions**

- **Ice Breaker Question:** If you could be any animal in the world, what would it be & why?

Lesson Time: (Suggested time: 30 minutes)

Lesson time will include the main points from the assigned reading for each chapter. (Note: Some chapters will be subdivided into two lessons.) Instructors can enhance lesson time by integrating personal stories and testimonials, additional scripture references, special guest speakers, etc.

- **Pgs. 77-83, Understanding the Abuse** – The focus of today's meeting is on uncovering what abuse is, defining it, and starting the discussion about the various types of abuse. Focus on the facts, the abuse, and the stories.

- *Abuse comes in several forms:* sexual, physical, emotional, and verbal.

- *EVERY form of abuse affects your overall well-being.* (Verbal and emotional abuse are NOT less significant than other abuses). Many people get over physical abuse before emotional abuse.

- *The way we are raised helps shape us and determines what we think about ourselves* – If we heard that we were fat, ugly, never going to amount to much, then at some point we began to believe it! We have to allow the truth of God's word to cleanse us and his truth of his word get deep within our souls.

- *Our parents sometimes didn't encourage us to talk about our feelings.* They pretend it doesn't exist. Feelings that aren't talked about are manifested – anger, addiction, abuse of our children, bad relationships. They never learned, but we can break the cycle.

- *Even in a "normal" home where abuse is not present, the lack of emotional support and verbal affirmation can begin to trigger women to make poor choices.* We start looking for love and affirmation in all the wrong places. We begin to look for what we are comfortable with. This means that if we were treated poorly in our home growing up, we will look for it in new relationships. We won't mean to, but we just will.

- *Many of us entered into an abusive relationship and it escalates slowly, where we didn't even realize it was happening.* Sometimes, it starts as control and manipulation. The abuser starts demanding "Don't go here. Don't wear that. Don't hang around with them." It escalates into a verbal assault. Then, the abuser starts saying "you are ugly, fat, lazy, no one wants you." Ultimately, it evolves in physical abuse. It slowly degrades your self-worth.

- *If a woman's self-worth is degraded, she begins to think that she doesn't deserve better.* If we enter into a relationship and someone is abusive – talking ugly, controlling, manipulating – then we'll likely stay a long time. We don't think we are worth more. This is why the abuser can often manipulate women into a dangerous or illegal situation, as well.

- *It almost always starts slowly* – a hair pull, a shove, pinning against the wall. It always escalates. We don't end it because we need him to give us value. We make excuses for the behavior. "He didn't mean to. He loves me. He's trying to do better. I just made him mad. It's my fault." Our value never comes from another human being. We are not who we are because someone told us. We are who we are because we were created for greatness by the creator of all things.

- *Sexual abuse is even harder.* There is so much shame attached to it. Only 25% of women report their sexual abuse. Sexual abuse comes in many forms: inappropriate touching, pornography, sexual acts in front of a child, sexual conversations. Childhood sexual abuse is usually non-violent because children are easy targets. As we age, we become numb. When entering adult relationships, we can even be raped and not speak up because we've been so desensitized.

- *Extended periods of abuse begin to show up in various ways:* excuses for behavior ("it's not that big of a deal"), bad music, bad relationships, parenting choices, addiction & crime. Shame, guilt, exhaustion and autoimmune diseases from stress can all manifest. The way we parent our children, the choices we make about future spouses, the job we take, and our overall sense of well-being can all be rooted in current or former abuse.

Group Discussion Time: (Suggested Time: 30 Minutes) Discuss questions from this week's homework located on pages 90-91.

Final thoughts: (5 minutes)

When we understand our self-worth, we will see yourself the way God sees us. The Lord is the everlasting God, the creator of all the earth. He never grows weak or weary. No one can measure the depths of his understanding. (Consider reading Psalm 91 over the moms.)

- **Homework Assignment for Next Meeting:** Read pages 84-89. Complete Week 2 discussion questions on pages 92-93.
- **Closing Prayer**

Ministry Leader Tips:

- Consider inviting someone in the church or community who has a powerful testimony of overcoming abuse to come and share for 15 minutes. (This could be you).
- Part I of Overcoming Abuse will focus on uncovering what abuse is, defining it, and starting the discussion about the various types of abuses. Keep it informative and be sure to focus on stories of recovery as told in the Bible, as well as testimonies of those you know. Part II will focus more on the recovery. What are some things that you can do for your own recovery? How can you

forgive those who have abused you? How can you prevent your children from being abused (or abused again)?

- Be sure to allot for extended prayer time. Have single moms break up into groups of two and pray for each other. If no abuse has occurred in a mom's life, encourage her to focus her prayers on someone she knows who has experienced such travesty.

- Be prepared to have referral resources available for severe issues that need extensive or immediate counseling. This can include counseling services in the community and in-patient treatment facilities, when necessary, as well as resources your church may have.

Overwhelmed Leader's Guide Meeting 2: Overcoming Abuse (Part II)

Food and Fellowship: (Suggested time: 30 minutes)

This time can be used for meal distribution, games, ice breakers, introduction, and opening prayer, taking care to make any new attendees feel welcome and having some fun. (Note: This can also include live worship or pre-recorded music).

- **Opening Prayer**

- **Welcome & Introductions**

- **Ice Breaker:** Tell one fun fact about yourself.

Lesson Time: (Suggested time: 30 minutes)

Lesson time will include the main points from the assigned reading for each chapter. (Note: Some chapters will be sub-divided into two lessons.) Instructors can enhance lesson time by integrating personal stories and testimonials, additional scripture references, special guest speakers, etc.

- **Pages 84-89, Healthy Healing** - The focus of today's meeting is on recognizing that healing is necessary in order to begin to thrive as a single mom. We'll also look at how to begin the healing process from past abuse.

- *Spend time healing* - There's too much at stake if we don't spend time healing. Often, we pretend it didn't happen or avoid talking about it. We might even say that it wasn't that big of a deal. However, if we do not spend time healing, we will become obsessed with the event(s). Our decisions will revolve around the abuse, and we will not be able to parent effectively. Every relationship going forward is ruined or tainted, and we will manipulate the relationship (subconsciously) so that we do not have to deal with the pain. We must actively pursue our own healing. It will not happen on its own. Remember, it's a process. Be kind to ourselves and give ourselves some grace to make mistakes and heal properly. Do not give up or give in. (Galatians 6:9). Do it for our children. Do it for ourselves.

- *You are not alone.* The percentage of women having suffered abuse has often been debated because so many women don't report abuse, especially when abuse can come in so many forms like we learned in our last meeting. The important thing to know is that we are not alone. We are not the only ones.

- *Embrace the need to be loved.* Our self-confidence and self-worth can often be tied to our need to be loved. One of the reasons we fall prey to abuse is because we've lost value in ourselves. We don't see ourselves the way God sees us. Therefore, we run to "false love" in places we can get it, tolerating abuses that should have never happened.

- *Forgiveness* – One of the important components of the healing process is in forgiveness. There's no mistaking that is likely the hardest part of the process. Forgiveness can include our perpetrator, enablers who have empowered the perpetrator, ourselves (and perception that it was somehow our fault), and even God. The forgiveness process will be just that – a process. It will be a daily choice to forgive. We may have to lay back at God's feet a thousand times before we begin to feel free from it. However, the critical part to know is that we are not free from it until we can forgive it. Important things to remember about forgiveness: a) It is not given because someone deserves it – just as Christ paid for our sins when we didn't deserve it. b) It does not excuse behavior. For example, when we are forgiven by God, it doesn't mean we don't have consequences. The forgiveness of a past abuser doesn't mean we indicate it's okay and certainly doesn't indicate we are seeking out a relationship with that person. c) Great freedom comes with forgiveness.

- *Counseling* – Seek out professional counseling if not done so already. Many churches have free or affordable counseling centers. There are also low-cost and sliding-scale counselors around the U.S., as well as Christian online counseling services. Once we begin to talk about it, we will begin to slowly feel that burden lifted from our shoulders. We may find that dealing with shame and healing from it is one of the most difficult things to do. Logically, we know the abuse is not our fault; we could not have prevented it. Even though we know that, we still tend to feel dirty, a feeling of not being "worthy" and, therefore, who would want us? This is shame and exactly what the enemy wants us to feel, but it is not the truth.

- *Strong prayer life* - Prayer is a very important part of recovery. There are things that no one else will probably understand, but God will. He is faithful. Get books on sexual healing from a Christian perspective. WE can read and then reread a section as many times as needed.

- *Mentor* – Get a mentor - someone who has gone through abuse and has recovered from it will be especially helpful. This person will help us stay accountable to following our recovery plan. She will also be a shoulder to cry on and a place of non-judgement with sound wisdom. Make sure to pray about who God would have this person be.

- *Stay connected.* Staying connected to this group will also provide a strong network of sisters who can pray and can help us along our healing journey.

Group Discussion Time: (Suggested Time: 30 minutes)
Discuss questions from this week's homework on pages 92-93.

Final thoughts: (5 minutes)
"Never be afraid to trust an unknown future to a known God." Corrie ten Boom"

- **Homework:** Read Chapter 8: Being a Single Parent & Complete Study Guide on pgs. 103-105
- **Closing Prayer**

Ministry Leader Tips:

- Refer to Ministry Leader notes on Week 2 on Overcoming Abuse: Part I.

Overwhelmed Leader's Guide Meeting 3: Being a Single Parent

Food and Fellowship: (Suggested time: 30 minutes)

This time can be used for meal distribution, games, ice breakers, introduction, and opening prayer, taking care to make any new attendees feel welcome and having some fun. (Note: This can also include live worship or pre-recorded music).

- **Opening Prayer**
- **Welcome & Introductions**
- **Ice Breaker:** Share three things that you have in common with your children. (hair color, eye color, outgoing, happy, funny, etc.)

Lesson Time: (Suggested time: 30 minutes)

Lesson time will include the main points from the assigned reading for each chapter. (Note: Some chapters will be sub-divided into two lessons.) Instructors can enhance lesson time by integrating personal stories and testimonials, additional scripture references, special guest speakers, etc.

- **Pages 95-102, Change can be difficult.** The focus of today's meeting is on being a single mom and how that changes the way that we may do some things. We also explore the key areas where single moms can struggle: finances, parenting, emotional stress, and pursuit of spiritual growth. We must be mindful of the counterfeits that come to fill a need that only God can.

- *Fruits of the Spirit allow us to parent well.* Only the Holy Spirit produces these kinds of fruits in our lives: love, joy, peace, patience, kindness, goodness, faithfulness, gentleness and self-control. Its only through the help of the Holy Spirit that can we achieve these fruits of the Spirit. We need all these fruits to do what God has called us to do.

- *Patience is necessary to parent well.* Often, single parenting didn't happen instantly. Whether we had an unexpected pregnancy or went through a treacherous divorce or a failed relationship, it is safe to say that having a baby that we must parent alone was not the plan for most of us. It takes time to undergo trauma and it will take time to heal from it. Patience is the key. Give ourselves time to go through the myriad of emotions we are undoubtedly experiencing. Allow time to regroup.

- *Love, peace, & joy will help us along the journey.* Love makes the world go around. In the middle of parenting a child alone and trying to stretch a dollar to put food on the table, can we even fathom love, peace and joy? And yet, we know John 14:27 promises us inexplicable peace that comes from Jesus. We may be trying to work three jobs to make ends meet. We don't know which way to turn. We are tired. However, joy can still be ours. Strengthening our relationship with the Lord through spiritual disciplines will allow us to continue to grow in these fruits.

- *Kindness & gentleness are fruits our children desperately need us to flourish in.* Has there been a time when parenting that we wished we had been a little more kind and gentle with our toddler or teenager? Do we ever wonder what is wrong with us? Are there other parents that scream profanities at their kids too? Ask God to help in this area.

- *Counterfeits can't fill the void.* Some of us have gone through our entire lives looking for the void in our heart to be filled. We have felt a hole. We have sought relationships that failed. We have been abandoned by family and friends. The church has failed to help give us value. However, when we look to another human being to be our source of joy and hope, we will always be disappointed. There is no man or woman on earth that can be perfect - no perfect friends, no perfect parents.

The hole in our heart can only be filled with Jesus Christ.

- *Evaluate emotional stress.* Becoming comfortable in the role of being a single parent will take some adjustment. We will go through many emotions, such as loneliness, fear, vulnerability, discouragement, anger, being overwhelmed, etc. We have to rely on our faith in the one who can deliver us. When we start replacing these emotions with scripture, our faith in God will increase. We will begin to experience unspeakable joy. There is nothing like it! We cannot make good decisions with high levels of emotional stress.

- *The pursuit of spiritual growth will change our parenting.* When we accept Jesus Christ into our lives as your Lord and Savior, it is when we truly start to live. The freedom experienced is life-changing. After this, will it always be roses and sunshine? No, of course not! Will we never have trouble? No. In John 16:33 Christ states, "I have told you these things, so that in me you may have peace. In this world, you will have trouble. But take heart! I have overcome the world." We will have hope that can make it through anything. We will have a peace that comes from deep within, not just some temporary high that we can get from things that won't fulfill us.

- *There are three main steps to becoming a Christian.* 1) Recognize what sin is. 2) Recognize that we are sinners and what the consequence of sin is. Repent of that sin. 3) Believe Jesus is the Son of God and the only way to God.

Group Discussion Time: (Suggested Time: 30 minutes)
Discuss questions from this week's homework on pages 95-102.

Final thoughts: (5 minutes)
We have to be whole in Christ and in nothing or no one else. It's not about religion, but having a relationship with Jesus. Jesus brings joy and peace despite what is going on around us.

- **Homework:** Read Chapter 9: Playing the Victim Role & Complete Study Guide (pgs. 115-117)
- **Closing Prayer**

Ministry Leader Tips:

- Talk to the ladies about the most significant challenges they have faced in their lives and how they overcame them. Have more experienced mothers share their success stories.

- Move the discussion to salvation. Be prepared to share the Gospel in its simplest form. Take your time with the presentation of the Gospel. Allow the Holy Spirit to minister. Discuss Galatians 5:22-23 and why salvation is important in the journey of single parenting.

- Close the discussion with the fruits of the spirit: love, joy, peace, patience, kindness, goodness, gentleness, and self-control. What do the moms see as the most important for their life? Why is the Holy Spirit's presence in their life crucial to achieving peace, for instance?

Overwhelmed Leader's Guide Meeting 4:
Playing the Victim Role (Part I)

Food and Fellowship: (Suggested time: 30 minutes)

This time can be used for meal distribution, games, ice breakers, introduction, and opening prayer, taking care to make any new attendees feel welcome and having some fun. (Note: This can also include live worship or pre-recorded music).

- **Opening Prayer**
- **Welcome & Introductions**
- **Ice Breaker:** If you could live in any sitcom, which one would it be?

Lesson Time: (Suggested time: 30 minutes)

Lesson time will include the main points from the assigned reading for each chapter. (Note: Some chapters will be subdivided into two lessons.) Instructors can enhance lesson time by integrating personal stories and testimonials, additional scripture references, special guest speakers, etc.

- **Pages 115-117, The Effects of Hurt** – The focus of today's meeting is on how past hurt, if not dealt with, will at some point immobilize us. It will ultimately define who we are as people, and how there are dozens of ways that we may have encountered situations in our lives that may have put us in a "victim role mentality."

- *Evaluate truth.* The Bible says that the truth sets us free and it is full of truth. There are times in our lives that it is easy to twist the truth to fit our situation or make it comfortable for us. We do this even with scripture, especially when we don't like what the truth really is. Truth is life. It is the litmus test that we run our decisions through.

- *Evaluate trauma.* Let's talk about hurt. There are dozens of ways we could have suffered trauma in our lives. (Examples can include: rape, molestation, physical or verbal abuse, alcoholic parent, divorce of your parents, or death, etc.) How we handle hurt is crucial to our future and the future of our children.

- *Be watchful for the danger zone.* There is an appropriate time to deal with the hurt. The Bible talks about us going through different seasons of life. It's healthy to mourn the loss of a loved one or to be angry or hurt if you have suffered abuse or were wronged at the hands of another person. When we get into the danger zone, however, is when we hold onto the hurt and are unable to move past it. Everyone's healing process will look different. The important thing is that you do work through it. (See examples on pages 108-109). Hurt generally has 3 stages: 1) It's nothing (when we deny we were even victimized), 2) it's everything (when we obsess over the occurrence), and 3) it's something (when we acknowledge it happened, but it no longer has control over us).

- *Immobilization can happen.* Until we deal with the events that hurt us, we will be immobilized. This will start to define who we are as a person. We become victims instead of the mom, sister, daughter, employee, etc. that God wants us to be.

- *It is easy to slip into the victim role when we've been hurt.* Instead of giving it to God, we get so caught up in wanting/needing to be right, to seek revenge, wanting someone to feel sorry for what has been done to us, that we become immobilized by it. We lose focus on the task at hand. The past consumes us. We cannot move forward.

- *Who does God say we are?* Negative thoughts can consume us. We may feel too fat, not pretty enough, not smart enough, not worthy enough, friend-less, hopeless, or misunderstood. It's hard, but we have to move past how we feel and replace that with the truth that God says about us or that will become your truth.

- *Job was a righteous man who faced major hardships.* Let's look at Job's life for a minute. He was a wealthy man and had a flourishing family and business. He was admired by his community and considered a God-fearing man. Suddenly, everything changed. Job lost it all (friends, family, health, wealth, and even respect). Can we relate to Job? Can we relate to the "suddenly" moment of his life? Job had two choices. He could praise God, or curse him. His choice of continuing to praise God ultimately set him free to experience more blessings than he even had before! Our praise will set us free!

Group Discussion Time: (Suggested Time: 30 minutes)
Discuss questions from this week's homework on pages 115-117.

Final thoughts: (5 minutes)
"Psalm 57:2 says "I will cry out to the God most high, to God who performs all things for me.""

- **Homework:** Read Chapter 9 and complete Study Guide (pgs. 118-119)

- Closing Prayer

Ministry Leader Tips:

- Discussing the victim mentality can be tricky for a leader. You want to handle each single mom with great compassion and sensitivity, as well as promote healing.
- The central theme in this chapter is about uncovering those things that can cause us to be victims. For example, did your spouse cheat on you? Have you suffered a life-threatening illness? Were you abused as a child? Whatever the challenge, most of us have faced many and it's important to acknowledge it, heal, and move on.
- Facilitate discussions around what the participants have faced, being sensitive to those things, but also then moving the discussion towards the healing process. How do we avoid camping out in the victim mentality? How do you avoid fostering such a mentality in your children?

Overwhelmed Leader's Guide Meeting 5: Playing the Victim Role (Part II)

Food and Fellowship: (Suggested time: 30 minutes)

This time can be used for meal distribution, games, ice breakers, introduction, and opening prayer, taking care to make any new attendees feel welcome and having some fun. (Note: This can also include live worship or pre-recorded music).

- Opening Prayer

- Welcome & Introductions

- **Ice Breaker:** If a movie was being made of your life and you could choose the actor/actress to play you, who would you choose and why?

Lesson Time: (Suggested time: 30 minutes)

Lesson time will include the main points from the assigned reading for each chapter. (Note: Some chapters will be sub-divided into two lessons.) Instructors can enhance lesson time by integrating personal stories and testimonials, additional scripture references, special guest speakers, etc.

- **Pages 118-119, Move from victim to victor.** The focus of today's meeting is on how sometimes it's easier to complain than actually do something to change the situation. It's okay to mourn the loss of a relationship, but we must keep going. We cannot blame God or others for our situation. We must move from victim to victor.

- *Sometimes it's easier to complain about our situation than to do anything about it.* It's like picking a scab over and over again and never healing from it. We cannot control the fact that we were wounded and experienced hardship, but we can control our response and how much power it has over our lives. It's important to begin the healing process which begins with talking about it. The discussion must be in a healthy way, however. "What was my role, if any?" "How does holding on to this cripple me?" "How will this impact my parenting if I don't forgive (myself, my ex, God, others)?" "How can I begin to take steps forward to move on with my life in a healthy way?"

- *Move on.* Yes, it's easier said than done. It is possible, though. It's okay to mourn the loss of a relationship or a death, but we must choose to get up and move on. Otherwise, depression, loneliness, suicidal thoughts, a feeling of inadequacy, self-pity, doubt, self-esteem issues, etc., can sneak up and overtake us. The only way we will lose the war is to give up. The only people who will suffer are our kiddos. It's too valuable a fight to just give up. We must stay in it and defeat the past lies in order to parent our children well and live a life that is meaningful, exciting, full, and expectant.

- *Avoid the blame game.* We have to be careful not to live blaming God or others for our situation. We have to be careful not to cause harm to the person who hurt us. Along with blaming others, sometimes we blame God as well. We will probably never be able to wrap our finite minds around why things happen in this life, but we can always turn to God's word. Isaiah 55:8-9 says," My thoughts are nothing like your thoughts and my ways are far beyond anything you could imagine. For just as the heavens are higher than the earth, so my ways are higher than your ways and my thoughts higher than your thoughts".

- *God is in control.* What God is saying is that he has it all under control. What we can be sure of is that "all things work together for the good of those who love the Lord and are called according to his purpose" (Romans

8:28). We must come to a place of peace with that fact in order to lose the victim mentality of "why did this happen?"

- *Our response is a choice.* We all wonder "why did this have to happen?" The truth is, it doesn't matter why. There is nothing that can be done about the past. God is sovereign and has a plan, even when bad things happen. The thing that we have control of is what we do with our future. We have to make the decision that we will not let anything from our past control us. It is a choice and one we can make daily.

- *God does truly work everything out for our good.* Even though this may not be evident to you now, you will, at some point, be able to speak into the lives of others who are or have gone through the same thing you have. Our testimonies are developed through the hardships we experience and the revelation that God delivered us from that, healed us, and set our feet on solid ground.

Group Discussion Time: (Suggested Time: 30 minutes)
Discuss questions from this week's homework on pages 118-119.

Final thoughts: (5 minutes)

"Watch your thoughts, they become words; watch your words, they become actions; watch your actions, they become habits; watch your habits, they become character; watch your character, for it becomes your destiny." ~ Author unknown

- **Homework:** Read Chapter 10: Parenting 101 & complete study guide (pgs. 134-138)
- **Closing Prayer**

Ministry Leader Tips:

- Refer to Ministry Leader notes on Week 5 on Playing the Victim Role: Part I

Overwhelmed Leader's Guide Meeting 6: Parenting 101 (Part I)

Food and Fellowship: (Suggested time: 30 minutes)

This time can be used for meal distribution, games, ice breakers, introduction, and opening prayer, taking care to make any new attendees feel welcome and having some fun. (Note: This can also include live worship or pre-recorded music).

- Opening Prayer
- Welcome & Introductions
- Ice Breaker: What song best describes you and why?

Lesson Time: (Suggested time: 30 minutes)

Lesson time will include the main points from the assigned reading for each chapter. (Note: Some chapters will be sub-divided into two lessons.) Instructors can enhance lesson time by integrating personal stories and testimonials, additional scripture references, special guest speakers, etc.

- **Pages 121-129, Assessing Key Parenting Questions & 4 Common Parenting Mistakes to Avoid.** The focus of today's meeting is on evaluating the key questions every single mom should be asking herself. We'll further explore the 4 common parenting mistakes single moms make and why we do it, including overindulging out of guilt, failing to discipline, being too strict, and negatively impacting our children's character through observation.

- **We want to see the fruit of our labor.** Good parenting takes effort. It is not easy. It is not free. It will not simply fall into our laps, but it is worth it! Every mom wants to be able to say, "I am very proud of my son/daughter." We envision the best for our children far more than we ever had. Even if we provide the best parenting we possibly can, there will be challenges. This is why we must keep the end goal in mind during the difficulties, especially when parenting through exhaustion. Proverbs 31:27-28 says, "She carefully watches everything in her household and suffers nothing to laziness. Her children stand and bless her." Our children will stand and bless us one day. (But remember, it will take much intention now before that ever happens. There will also be some difficult days, when we see little fruit of our labor. That's normal and does not mean we have failed!)

- **We need to ask ourselves hard questions.** The biggest components to effective parenting are by assessing some critical questions in our lives. Yes, our parenting starts with us. There are 4 key questions we need to have foundational answers to in order to be the most effective parents.

- **Question 1: *Do I have a relationship with Jesus?*** Do we understand what that means? If we are currently in a single moms' Bible study in our church, it is likely we know of Jesus. We've likely even heard the gospel, but do we walk intimately with him daily? Do you know him and his unfailing love? Do we talk with him, praying without ceasing? Is he a friend – an ever-present help in times of trouble? The more we grow in a relationship with Jesus, understanding the sacrifice he made for us and the love he has for us, the more we grow as parents. When we understand the love of our Heavenly Father, it shifts our parenting. This is the foundation from which all else will flow. This relationship can't be forsaken with an expectation that our parenting will somehow work itself out. Take the time to forge true relationship with the King and understand that our parenting load will be easier. (His yoke is easy, and burden is light).

- **Question 2: *Do I feel good enough?*** Do we feel worthy of love? If the answer is *no*, then we will have a hard time imparting positive parenting to our children. Insecurity, self-doubt, feelings of inadequacy, and low self-worth can often be attributed to trauma we experienced as single mothers. Whether it was the heartache of a failed relationship, death, or past abuse, when trauma has been experienced, lingering effects can be feelings of unworthiness. These feelings, when not strongly assessed, evaluated, and work on, can become the lens in which we parent. It causes us to raise children who, also, don't feel they are good enough. We must come to a place of understanding our worth through Christ and the healing transformational power of a relationship with him in order to parent healthy.

- *Question 3: Am I happy where I am right now?* Philippians 4:11-13 (NLT) says, "Not that I was ever in need, for I have learned how to be content with whatever I have. I know how to live on almost nothing or with everything. I have learned the secret of living in every situation, whether it is with a full stomach or empty, with plenty or little. For I can do everything through Christ, who gives me strength." The circumstances that exist in our lives today may not have been what we planned for a variety of reasons. We may have long days and big obstacles, but the secret to contentment is learning to embrace every season and finding joy in it. Do we want to raise children who are full of joy, excited for their futures, and overcomers despite difficult obstacles? If so, then we must exhibit that for them.

Learn to embrace the joys of the day, living in gratitude for the blessings we have – good health, provision, a church family, beautiful children, and the list goes on.

- *Question 4: Do I believe God put dreams inside me?* Am I taking steps to realize them and live them out? The best thing we can do to teach our children to achieve their dreams is to achieve our own. As moms, we often lay down our dreams when we have children. And yes, those dreams may shift some as our responsibilities have shifted, but it's important to take time to evaluate the dreams God has placed in our hearts. Did he call you to write a book? Launch a business? Finish your degree or high school equivalency? Start a bible study? Serve in vacation bible school? There are many possibilities, both big and small. Take time to write down the things God has whispered in our hearts long ago and make an action plan on how to achieve them. Maybe it's a tiny step each week or month. We don't have to do it all at once but show our children that all things are possible with Christ Jesus.

- *There are 4 common parenting mistakes that we make as single parents (or married parents, for that matter!)* Parenting takes intentionality and, to be honest, sometimes we overlook things due to the load on our plates. Let's take a look at four of the most common mistakes we can make as single moms.

- **Common Parenting Mistake 1: Overindulgence out of guilt.** This is the most common of all the parenting mistakes. We carry guilt from our single parenting experience – any past mistakes we have made, the guilt of working two jobs, the guilt of dad not living in the home, or the guilt that we have to work multiple jobs leaving little room for down-time and play time. There could be many reasons for the guilt, but when left unaddressed, it may cause us to overindulge our children's wants. Examples of this can include buying our children items we cannot afford or giving permission to participate in activities we aren't comfortable with. These feelings can cause massive amounts of overindulgence, including lack of boundaries, failure to discipline, and excusing our children's inappropriate behavior. This doesn't help our children. There must be balance. Loving our children is in being strong enough to say no, when needed. We don't want our children growing up ill-prepared for life as a result.

- **Common Parenting Mistake 2: Failing to discipline.** The reason we sometimes fail to discipline could be from exhaustion, fear of constantly being the bad guy, or maybe uncertainty of how to discipline. Whatever the reason, we must discipline! All good parents do, even our Heavenly Father. Remember, our children crave structure and right discipline from a very young age, but it's never too late to start. Understanding how to establish boundaries that work for our homes, sticking to those boundaries, and delivering consequences are all important steps to teaching our children life principles and keeping them safe and healthy.

- *Common Parenting Mistake 3: Being too strict may lead to rebellion.* The complete opposite of failing to discipline is being too strict. While we do not want to be a pushover parent, we also don't want to be a bully parent either. While some parents overindulge and overcompensate out of guilt, other parents can swing the pendulum too far to the opposite side and parent with no leniency, no grace, and little compassion. Many parents do this out of fear that their children will get too wild, become just another statistic, or will have long-term residual effects of a one-parent households. While those concerns are important to be mindful of, it is also critical that we parent like our Heavenly Father. There are consequences for behaviors, but there is also grace. There is grace and room to fail without WWIII happening. Be careful with pushing our children too hard. Have fun with them. Issue grace. Laugh with them.

- **Common Parenting Mistake 4: Negatively impacting our child's character.** Similar to pursuing and achieving our dreams, this parenting mistake has to do with our children's observations about how we behave. They will likely emulate what we do, not what we say. That said, it's important we evaluate what we do, including our media consumption. A good question we must ask ourselves often is, "Would I be comfortable with my children watching this program with me?" What we feed our spirit becomes what we think. What we think becomes what we do. What we do becomes how we feel. And what we feel can become our character. Other evaluations need to be our commitment to honesty in our homes, sexual morality, and prejudices against others.

- **Do not dwell on the inadequacies.** We may not be living the life we once envisioned. We should learn to embrace where we are right now, enjoying our children and enjoying who God is and who he's made us to be. Be the mom they need now. Enjoy your season.

Group Discussion Time: (Suggested Time: 30 minutes)
Discuss questions from this week's homework on pages 134-136.

Final thoughts: (5 minutes)

The foundation of good parenting is first in surrendering ourselves to our Heavenly Father, committing to grow in him daily, and learning through his word and example how to parent. Further, we must evaluate the core questions that ensure our own emotional and spiritual health first. It is through our own health that we are able to parent effectively. And finally, we must avoid the common mistakes that parents make, including being aware of the pitfalls we can succumb to and being strong in our boundaries and discipline. As we remind ourselves that too much is at stake, we become stronger and more confident in our parenting.

- **Homework:** Complete study guide in Chapter 10 (pgs. 136-138)
- **Closing Prayer**

Ministry Leader Tips:

- Discuss the four hard questions. This will allow single moms of different life stages to speak candidly about what God is doing in their heart. They can share about their dreams, joys, and growth in Christ. Be certain to bring the discussion back to why these questions are important to answer as a mom.

- Next, focus on the four common parenting mistakes made by single parents. Direct discussions towards why these are mistakes and how to work through them once recognized. Feel free to share about your own parenting failures. This will allow other moms the freedom to share theirs.

- For a more in-depth look at parenting well as a single mom, you will want to check out *Kids and the Single Mom: A Real-World Guide to Effective Parenting*. It's a continuation of our single parenting curriculum.

Overwhelmed Leader's Guide Meeting 7: Parenting 101 (Part II)

Food and Fellowship: (Suggested time: 30 minutes)

This time can be used for meal distribution, games, ice breakers, introduction, and opening prayer, taking care to make any new attendees feel welcome and having some fun. (Note: This can also include live worship or pre-recorded music).

- **Opening Prayer**
- **Welcome & Introductions**
- **Ice Breaker:** Tell us your funniest parenting story or something cute you remember your children doing.

Lesson Time: (Suggested time: 30 minutes)

Lesson time will include the main points from the assigned reading for each chapter. (Note: Some chapters will be sub-divided into two lessons.) Instructors can enhance lesson time by integrating personal stories and testimonials, additional scripture references, special guest speakers, etc.

- **Pages 130-134, Five Steps to Make us a Better Mom.** There are five key steps that will help us along our parenting journey as we evaluate the common parenting mistakes and how to avoid them. We must recognize our need for others, ensure self-care is implemented, communicate with our children, achieve our dreams, and serve others. We'll evaluate each one and how they make us better parents.

- *Recognize that we need help.* We cannot do it alone. Do not be prideful. Ask for help when needed. Ecclesiastes 4:9-10 says, "Two people are better off than one, for they can help each other succeed. If one person falls, the other can reach out and help." Single mom support groups can be critical in building a tribe that can help us overcome. Our support circles may look different as we may or may not have physical family. However, single mom support groups can provide that spiritual family that is necessary to grow as individuals and, also, act as a support to one another.

- *Allow for some alone time.* This may seem impossible, but it is crucial. We must have time to regroup for our own mental health and emotional well-being. There has to be a quiet time for prayer. Quiet time may be limited due to demands on our schedules, but all of us can take 15 minutes a day several times a week. Maybe that alone time is soaking in the tub after the children are in bed or before they awake in the morning. Maybe it's a face mask and chocolates while hiding in the pantry! It's all about being intentional with your alone time to breathe and to also experience time with the Lord. Consider taking some time once or twice per month to meet with a friend, mentor, or counselor. If childcare is an issue, find a babysitting co-op in your area or create a group of girlfriends who take turns babysitting for each other, such as in your single moms' group. We cannot avoid this parenting step! Stress can mount causing us to be unfair with our children or even raise our voices or strike in anger. Self-care is critical.

- *We need to talk to our kids.* As children grow, they need verbal affirmation from their parents. They need to hear they are doing a great job. We often don't find this difficult when they are small, and we provide accolades while they potty train or take their first steps. However, as they age and parenting challenges arise, we sometimes get so busy troubleshooting that we often forget to voice praise for our children. It's important we look for something to praise them for. Do not offer false praise! Look for something that our children are doing well and speak to that. Also, speak to the greatness we see inside them, even if we don't see the fruit yet. Further, we must also have open dialogue, age-appropriate, communication with our children. No subject is off-limits as they age. Sex, finances, personal hygiene, and spiritual growth need to be taught in the home first. Be bold and open the door of communication early. Keep it open. Be mindful of how we communicate with our children. We should avoid using foul language or screaming. If we feel anger rising, walk away immediately. This form of verbal abuse can scar our children for years to come.

- ***We should not lose our dreams.*** As discussed in Part I of our Parenting 101 chapter, dreaming again is a key part of the life experience. We should not allow life to beat us down to a point where we forget our dreams. Disappointments, failures, and fear are all a part of the journey, but not the end result. We have a purpose. Our children have a purpose. God has plans for our lives. Jeremiah 29:11 says, "For I know the plans I have for you,' says the Lord. 'They are plans for good and not disaster, to give you a future and a hope.'" The best thing we can do for our children's dreams is to achieve our own. Our children have dreams as well. Encourage them and foster an environment that allows them to thrive. We should build them up by speaking positively over them and the greatness we see in them.

- *We can make a difference in our community.*
  Volunteering is a rewarding experience and offers a new perspective. There is always someone who is worse off than us, so serving others gives us the opportunity to meet a need. Further, research indicates that service above self releases a greater sense of self-worth. We all can do something. There is always someone to serve. Volunteering will take our minds away from our own problems and will allow us to reach out to others. Further, it is a great principle to teach our children. Get children involved in the fun. Service doesn't have to be complicated. It can be serving food at a local food bank or joining in the mission of a local church or nonprofit. It can also be baking cookies for service workers, creating care packages for nursing home residents, or mowing the lawn of a neighbor. The list of possibilities is endless.

- *Embrace the journey.* The life we lead may not be the one we envisioned for ourselves or for our children, and that is perfectly okay. We should embrace where we are right now. Enjoy our children. Enjoy who God has made us to be, and trust that we have been given these children to raise because he knew we could do it and do it well.

Group Discussion Time: (Suggested Time: 30 minutes)

Discuss questions from this week's homework on pages 136-138.

Final thoughts: (5 minutes)

Who can we lean on to help us with parenting? Are there mentors, other single moms, or our own parents that can offer wise counsel and a listening ear? Be intentional about developing a tribe. Additionally, take time this week to schedule some alone time. It doesn't have to be a full day at the spa. 15 minutes in a bathroom alone with a hot shower running and a face mask on can make meaningful impact into a busy life. Learn to embrace the journey with intention, joy, and laughter.

- **Homework:** Read Chapter 11 Surviving Financial Crisis & Complete study guide (pgs. 159-160)
- **Closing Prayer**
-

Ministry Leader Tips:

- Consider inviting one or more single moms to share testimonials of parenting trials that have been overcome with intention.
- Also, this may be a great time to pass out volunteer opportunities that may exist in your community the group can perform together or individually. The group

can even create their own service project as a way to give back to your church or community.

Overwhelmed Leader's Guide Meeting 8: Surviving Financial Crisis (Part I)

Food and Fellowship: (Suggested time: 30 minutes)

This time can be used for meal distribution, games, ice breakers, introduction, and opening prayer, taking care to make any new attendees feel welcome and having some fun. (Note: This can also include live worship or pre-recorded music).

- **Opening Prayer**
- **Welcome & Introductions**
- **Ice Breaker:** If you had a million dollars, what would you do with it? Be as specific and detailed as possible. Allow yourself to dream a little.

Lesson Time: (Suggested time: 30 minutes)

Lesson time will include the main points from the assigned reading for each chapter. (Note: Some chapters will be sub-divided into two lessons.) Instructors can enhance lesson time by integrating personal stories and testimonials, additional scripture references, special guest speakers, etc.

- **Pages 139-150, Ways to Survive a Financial Crisis.** The focus of today's meeting is on the importance of financial health and some of the key components of achieving and maintaining financial health, including a deeper look at tithing and budgeting.

- *Financial crisis is common among single mothers.* Yep, this is certainly not a shocker for most of us, right?! Whether one arrived at single parenthood through death of a spouse, divorce, unplanned pregnancy, or other, it is likely the financial situation in the home shifted upon arrival to the single parenting journey. Financial crisis can come in many forms, including unplanned expenses, failure to plan and prepare, financial literacy, and lack of future plans, among others. As with any improvement, financial improvement will take time, intention, and integration of key principles. Let's look at two.

- *"If only I had more money, life would not be so difficult."* This is likely a thought we've had or a concern we've voiced many times. However, take a look at Matthew 25:23. "His master replied, 'Well done, good and faithful servant! You have been faithful with a few things; I will put you in charge of many things. Come and share your master's happiness!'" It's important that we steward what we have in our hand, whether little or much. The challenges you face financially today may not be your own doing. Perhaps you carry debt from an ex-spouse or were abandoned as a stay-at-home mom. Finances can be complex and the challenges multi-layered, but the important thing is in stewarding what you do have well. The first step in stewardship is tithing.

- **Tithing can change our financial picture....and our heart.** Tithing may be a new thing for us. Let's look at this principle in Scripture. (See Genesis 14:20, Leviticus 27:30, Deuteronomy 14:22, Malachi 3:10.) Tithing means "tenth" and requires us to give 10% of our income back to the Lord (through a local church). This can be difficult for different reasons - when finances are already tight, when we question if the church will steward the dollars correctly, or if this is our first exposure to this Biblical principle. However, tithing is about a surrendered heart.

- **Tithing isn't about God needing our money.** It's about us needing God to bless our money. It's about surrendering control of our finances to him, as we recognize we owe everything to him anyway. Tithing is recognizing that he can do more with the 90% remaining than we could with the 100% without his blessing. 2 Corinthians 9:7-8 says, "And don't give reluctantly or in response to pressure. For God loves a person who gives cheerfully and God will generously provide all we need. Then, we will always have everything we need and plenty left over to share with others". This is a test of our faith and obedience. For those who would argue that tithing is an Old Testament principle no longer required of Christians, my response often is, "We cannot out-give God. He's already given so much." While I'm not a Biblical scholar or theologian, I'll simply say that as a single mom who once robbed my children's piggy banks to scrape coins to put gas in the car, I know what it is to have nothing. Further, I know what it is to see God do the miraculous. We cannot afford not to tithe. The Lord will bless the surrender and give us wisdom on how to steward the remainder. God is our provider, not man, not the government, and not even our jobs. God can use those things, of course, but as we shift heart perspective to surrender it all to him and learn to steward it well, he will bless the effort.

- *Relinquish fear from your money.* We often do not tithe because we fear we won't have enough. In fact, the poverty mentality is one that many single parents suffer with (and many beyond single parenting as well). The fear that we will never have enough is often rooted in past money woes or other trauma. However, God is faithful, and his system is not the world's money system. He calls us into trust with him that he may do the supernatural. This may be meals showing up on your doorstep unexpectedly, a check coming in the mail from a source you didn't even know was owed to you, a bill inexplicably getting paid by a stranger, an unscheduled pay raise or bonus, or any of a number of other ways.

- *The second principle we need to explore this week is budgeting.* Budgeting is necessary in money management. Budgeting, in its simplest form, is simply knowing what income and debt is flowing in and out of our homes, then making a plan on how to move the needle forward, based on evaluation of that information. Such as with any self-improvement, e.g. weight loss, self-care, or the like, financial literacy and health takes time, intention, and practice. Many of us weren't taught strong financial principles and likely have had to learn through trial and error. Further, single parenting often brings a shift in household finances that require nothing short of a miracle of God to handle. The great news?! He's in the miracle-making business.

- *There are countless free online tools to assist in budget development.* There are free income calculators, debt management tools, and budget templates. Or…. simply start a list of all the bills owed, including interest rates, balances, and monthly payments on a sheet of paper. Then, list monthly income. Commit to thirty days of tracking every expense, including purchases for toiletries, entertainment, beauty, and others. Be diligent. At the end of the month, we should be able to assess our financial situation clearly.

- *Budgeting includes living within our means.* This may be a significant shift to your life prior to single parenting, and there's no doubt that change isn't fun. Living within your means may include downsizing homes or apartments, relocating into a lesser expensive community, trading in a current automobile, and/or re-evaluating education, entertainment, and clothing purchases in the home, just to name a few.

- *Evaluate potential savings opportunities in our budget.* Compare monthly obligations with what is actually spent and see where there is opportunity to save money, if possible. Did we buy 4 cups of coffee at a coffee shop that equated to 4x what it would cost to brew at home? Did we spend money on beauty that could be done at home? Did we overspend on food, including work lunches that could have been cooked at home? We'll explore savings opportunities in more depth in the next meeting, including couponing and rebates.

- *Begin to work with a financial education instructor.*
  Develop a game plan to reduce debt, increase income, and develop an emergency savings account. There are great programs, such as Crown Financial, Dave Ramsey, and Thrive Financial that provide faith-based, financial instruction at low cost. (Some churches even offer scholarships for those programs). Further, Single Mom University has a number of single parent-centric courses on financial education, including top financial tips every single parent should know, 25 ways to save money, and much more. Check that out at www.SingleMomUniversity.com.

Group Discussion Time: (Suggested Time: 30 minutes)
Discuss questions from this week's homework on pages 159-160.

Final thoughts: (5 minutes)
Thomas Edison once said, "Opportunity is missed by most people because it is dressed in overalls and looks like work." It will take work to rectify a difficult financial picture, but it is possible. These will be times of growth and challenge, but they will also be times of great revelation of how good God is and his provision over our lives. Testimonies will come from the financial hardships.

- **Homework Assignment for Next Meeting:** Complete Study Guide (pgs.161-163).
- **Closing Prayer**

Ministry Leader Tips:

- This is difficult and a common struggle faced by single mothers at some point throughout the single parenting journey. To deny that it is hard to raise children on one income would not be realistic. However, we know God's provision is not limited by our circumstances and it is not limited to just spiritual gifts. He provides in a variety of ways, physically, emotionally, parenting, spiritually, and financially. Take time to evaluate additional tools that can serve the mothers through financial workshops, workbooks, free internet resources, books, and tools in the community.
- This may be a great week to invite a guest speaker to come in and share on finances. Suggestions include: a banker at your local bank, a business owner in the church, or someone certified to do financial planning in your community.
- Consider helping each attendee to develop a budget through a budget-making exercise. This can include

having them bring a list of debt and income. They can work privately or in groups.

Overwhelmed Leader's Guide Meeting 9: Surviving Financial Crisis (Part II)

Food and Fellowship: (Suggested time: 30 minutes)

This time can be used for meal distribution, games, ice breakers, introduction, and opening prayer, taking care to make any new attendees feel welcome and having some fun. (Note: This can also include live worship or pre-recorded music).

- **Opening Prayer**
- **Welcome & Introductions**
- **Ice Breaker:** Would you rather be the funniest or smartest person in the room? Why?

Lesson Time: (Suggested time: 30 minutes)

Lesson time will include the main points from the assigned reading for each chapter. (Note: Some chapters will be sub-divided into two lessons.) Instructors can enhance lesson time by integrating personal stories and testimonials, additional scripture references, special guest speakers, etc.

- **Pages 151–158, Financial evaluation and accountability is necessary.** The focus of today's meeting is on the importance of evaluating and understanding our credit report, the value of coupons and discounts, and finally assessing the emotions we link to money and how that can positively or negatively impact our single parenting experience.

- *Credit scores impact more areas of our lives than we may have realized.* Our credit score evaluation can be linked to future purchases, such as a home or car, but can also drive up or down the interest rate we pay on such purchases. It can impact the rates we pay for credit cards or other debt, as well. Credit scores can be utilized by landlords to determine whether we can even rent in a particular building, as well. Credit scores can be pulled in conjunction with application for employment to ascertain an applicant's character, stewardship, and more. Automobile and homeowner's insurance can also drive rates based on credit scoring of clients. These are just a few of the ways a credit score can impact your future. This is why we must not ignore our credit scores, even if the picture today isn't what we want it to be. We take it one step at a time.

- *First, we begin with assessing our current credit score.* Monitoring our credit report will help build up our credit score. We are entitled to one free credit report, per year, per U.S. government guidelines. Take advantage and order it. Understanding your credit history, including incorrect data that may be reported, debt load that may have been forgotten, and credit scores will assist in making future plans, about to rectify any difficult situations. While reducing debt may not be an option today, due to limited income and tight budgets, it's important that we analyze our financial picture. We are women of integrity who will pay what we owe. We will be disciplined spenders who live within our means, recognizing the pedicure can wait when necessary.

- *Next, we make a plan for improvement.* This process will likely be slow, but be intentional. When paying off debt, there are a few things to consider. First, pay off the smallest debts first. This will improve credit score more quickly as you reduce debt load, but will also fuel a sense of accomplishment. Next, focus on high interest rate debts. Talk with creditors to ascertain possible settlements or reductions in interest rates or other negotiations.

- *Co-signing is a recipe for disaster.* Psalm 37:21 says "The wicked borrow and never repay, but the righteous give generously." Don't be manipulated into co-signing for a boyfriend, family member, coworker or other, who does not have acceptable credit. This is a danger zone that will likely leave you holding the bag in the future. Further, do not lend credit or debit cards for a charge that they promise to pay back. When keeping future financial goals in mind, including reducing debt, developing an emergency savings, and planning for retirement and children's educational expenses, we certainly cannot afford to take on another's debt. Moms, guard yourselves! Be careful not to allow emotions to entangle us in a financial catastrophe. Ultimately, we are responsible for any purchases made in our name.

- *Coupons and discounts can save you money.* Become a diligent detective at discovering rebates, coupons, and discounts. Where are the weekly kids-eat-free deals in your community? What grocery stores run sales and on what days? What grocery stores offer price-matching or other special purchase deals? What websites may offer great coupon codes, discounts, or insight on money-saving tips? There is a wealth of information out there on ways to save significant dollars of everyday household items and services. Commit to doing some research. Gather some of your single mom friends to share ideas. Coupon while watching your favorite television program. Get the kids involved. There are significant savings available, simply by doing some research. Many large purchases do include rebates, such as car batteries or automobiles, but some do not follow up with the paperwork necessary to get the money back. These are simple ways that can save thousands to be utilized on debt reduction or other financial plans.

- *Evaluating emotions linked to money is the final step in making sure you steward future dollars well.* Emotional spending and impulse buying are caused by an underlying issue. 2 Timothy 1:7 says, "God hasn't given us a spirit of fear, but of power, love and a sound mind." We do not have to fear our finances. Fear can drive over-spending. Over-spending can be a coping mechanism, just as alcoholism or drug use can. It can be a futile attempt at finding peace. Yet, we know, ultimately, it will result in more stress.

- *Additional tips for solid money management are as follows:* Do not spend without a budget. Do not spend to self-medicate. Do not over-indulge children from guilt of an absentee parent (buying items we cannot afford to appease them). Do not let past failures determine future financial spending. Do not ignore credit history. Take small steps daily to rectify financial situations. Procure a second job if necessary, including work-from-home or at-home sales positions.

- *Freedom is possible with due diligence.* Financial freedom, like any other freedom for that matter, takes discipline, self-control, diligence, commitment, persistence, and time. It takes a commitment to education and long-term planning and effort, but it is not God's intention to leave you drowning with no support. In Isaiah 43:2-3, he promises that we will not drown nor be consumed by difficulty. Keep pushing.

Group Discussion Time: (Suggested Time: 30 minutes)
Discuss questions from this week's homework on pages 161-163

Final thoughts: (5 minutes)
"You must gain control over your money or the lack of it will forever control you." ~ Dave Ramsey, Financial Peace University. It is important that we take the steps necessary to gain control over our finances. We will not be bound in fear in any area of our life, when we are actively engaged in the process of improvement, prayer, and commitment.

- **Homework Assignment for Next Meeting:** Read Chapter 12: Cycles and complete questions on page 173-174
- **Closing Prayer**

Ministry Leader Tips:

- Identify 5 possible websites or resources where attendees can learn more about saving money. (Hint: There are a number of money saving articles on The Life of a Single Mom's website).
- Research couponing websites.
- Create a contest where attendees can bring in coupons. The mom who brings the most coupons in wins a door prize. Host a couponing party.
- Challenge members to bring in 3 tips to save money and create a binder for all attendees with the tips.
- Make discussions about finances fun. Opening the door to healthy financial discussions allows for a release of pressure that many attendees may be feeling. Also, attendees may pick up tips from other single moms while in the group.
- Testimonials are especially helpful during these meetings.

Overwhelmed Leader's Guide Meeting 10: Here We Go 'Round the Mulberry Bush' - Cycles

Food and Fellowship: (Suggested time: 30 minutes)

This time can be used for meal distribution, games, ice breakers, introduction, and opening prayer, taking care to make any new attendees feel welcome and having some fun. (Note: This can also include live worship or pre-recorded music).

- **Opening Prayer**
- **Welcome & Introductions**
- **Ice Breaker:** If you were famous, what would you be famous for?

Lesson Time: (Suggested time: 30 minutes)

Lesson time will include the main points from the assigned reading for each chapter. (Note: Some chapters will be sub-divided into two lessons.) Instructors can enhance lesson time by integrating personal stories and testimonials, additional scripture references, special guest speakers, etc.

- **Pages 165-172, Here We Go 'Round the Mulberry Bush' - Cycles.** The focus of today's meeting is on what cycles are commonly identified in a single parent home, and how we can break them. Further, we explore how being raised in a dysfunctional family where there was abuse, alcoholism, or a whole myriad of other things does not mean we are destined to repeat the cycle. We have the power, through Christ, to create a new future for our children.

- *What are cycles?* Cycles are a series of events that are regularly repeated in the same order; a complete set or series. Examples can include cyclical abuse, cyclical poverty, cyclical sexual immorality, divorce, and more.

- *Our parents' choices greatly impact our future choices.* Often, people who struggle with alcoholism, addiction, pornography, obesity, and a number of other challenges, have also witnessed those same struggles in the generation before through parents and even grandparents. Repeating the cycle is not planned, but it happens. Without intentionality, we can repeat the cycle. The good news is that, with intentionality, we can break it.

- *Cycles destroy our future and our hope for tomorrow.* They limit us from seeing where we can go because we only see where we came from. Cycles usually start slow.

Over time, verbal, physical, and emotional abuse, that started with only one harsh word, has morphed into a dangerous situation. Likewise, addiction, sexual promiscuity, or over-spending may have started with one action, then two, and over time, patterns form. It's critical to recognize these patterns and be mindful of decisions we're making in our parenting and why we make these decisions.

- **Parents often avoid talking to their children about sex.** Sexual sin is one of the strongest bondages affecting God's people today. It holds us hostage. Yet, many homes avoid the subject altogether or simply say, "don't do it." This methodology is ineffective if we hope to break patterns of behavior that we may have seen or done. Open dialogue and communication, early and often, is critical. Exploring God's word, along with testimonials, prayer, and candor, will help children understand the *why* behind the *no.*

- **Movies and TV glamorize sexual immorality to make it appealing to the viewer.** The focus is on promoting that anything goes and to do what feels right. Our children are exposed to this early. The data is staggering on the challenges faced by our children and even, potentially their children. The challenges of sexual immorality, beyond dishonoring the Lord with our bodies, include depression, loneliness, insecurity, and trauma that remains after making the poor choices. Yet we still continue to pursue this bondage because we don't understand how clearly it affects our bodies, including our mental health. So how do we stop this?

- *First, we must recognize that we are in the midst of a potential cycle.* This can be the hardest part. Many times, we see our parents get abused or be the abuser. We see them become alcoholics, so we fear that it is going to be us in twenty years. If not careful, we condition ourselves to expect less of our futures. We begin to expect that cycle, that it is somehow our lot in life, but the blood of Christ breaks every chain through prayer, good decisions, and discernment.

- *When we accept Christ, we are a new creation.* 2 Corinthians 5:17 says, "this means that anyone who belongs to Christ has become a new person, the old life is gone, and the new life has begun." This is good news for all of us! But what happens when we mess up a week later, months later, or year later? (Hint: We will). The Bible says Gods mercy is new every morning. We ask God for forgiveness, for strength to make a better choice in the future, and turn from our ways. And we might have to do it again and again. However, freedom in Christ is always a much easier weight to carry than the heavy burdens of sin and cycles. It is for freedom that Christ set us free. We want to teach our children that we are not bound by our pasts or the pasts of our parents. We are free to make choices that honor the Lord and his blessings are far better than a temporary pleasure that will soon fade.

Group Discussion Time: (Suggested Time: 30 minutes)
Discuss questions from this week's homework on pages 173-174.

Final thoughts: (5 minutes)
It is of the utmost importance to think about what we're thinking about. We have the freedom to make new decisions. We are no longer bound to the bondage of who or what we once were. We decide the outcome of our life now. Choose life.

- **Homework Assignment for Next Meeting:** Read Chapter 13: Whom the Son sets free... (Pgs.177-195).
- **Closing Prayer**

Ministry Leader Tips:

- What are the cycles that we often perpetuate in our homes? Alcoholism? Abuse? Sexual immorality? Profanity? There are dozens of answers. Focus on the things that have been true in the homes of single mothers in your group. Take a closer look at those things that our parents were, our grandparents, and so on. It is important to uncover issues that took place in the childhood of our participants. Oftentimes, cycles started there. Did a grandfather say something that the participant held onto as their truth? Was their abuse that started early on? Can participants begin to see any cycles that have started in their families, that they have duplicated in their children's lives?

- Now is the time to talk about sexual sin. This chapter details the statistics on why sex outside of marriage can cause big problems and it also looks at Biblical teaching on the subject. Don't shy away from this one. Share with wisdom and compassion, offering a listening ear to your single mom group attendees. It's important that they feel the group is a safe space to share and receive healing. Freedom can be found in this environment, so don't rush through the hard discussions.

Overwhelmed Leader's Guide Meeting 11: Whom the Son Sets Free (Part I)

Food and Fellowship: (Suggested time: 30 minutes)

This time can be used for meal distribution, games, ice breakers, introduction, and opening prayer, taking care to make any new attendees feel welcome and having some fun. (Note: This can also include live worship or pre-recorded music).

- Opening Prayer
- Welcome & Introductions
- **Ice Breaker:** If we could hang out with any cartoon character, who would we choose and why?

Lesson Time: (Suggested time: 30 minutes)

Lesson time will include the main points from the assigned reading for each chapter. (Note: Some chapters will be sub-divided into two lessons.) Instructors can enhance lesson time by integrating personal stories and testimonials, additional scripture references, special guest speakers, etc.

- **Pages 177-187, Whom the Son Sets Free.** The focus of today's meeting is on how important is it to be free in all aspects of our lives and on how to give and receive forgiveness! We'll explore what bondage looks like and what freedom looks like in our lives.

- *Freedom offers us the confidence to persevere.* As we come to the end of our journey together in the Overwhelmed study, we are going to discuss freedom! This can be an exciting topic, or a scary one, as we explore challenges we may face from old wounds, heavy bondage, and the weights that come with that bondage. The Overwhelmed study is about giving a variety of tools that every single mom can use in various seasons and circumstances, but all the tools hinge on freedom. Freedom is necessary to be empowered. Victory is ours, but we cannot experience it if we are tied to heavy chains of our pasts, our trauma, or stinkin' thinkin'!

- *Freedom in Christ is the tie that binds every area together.* As we've built on every lesson including parenting, finances, abuse, navigating new seasons, and avoiding cycles, we land at the freedom of choice. We are free to choose bondage or a wide-open, expansive life that Christ paid for us to have. Freedom is necessary to parent effectively, manage finances well, and to relinquish control of fears and doubts. Freedom is bought and paid for, but it must be pursued.

- *We live in one of two places, either bondage or freedom.* There is no halfway point. We do not straddle the fence with one leg in freedom and the other in bondage. If you are free, you are not halfway free, or partly free, you are completely free. Otherwise, you live in bondage. Bondage vary widely from person to person and can be attributed to many causes, including parental relationships, abuse, trauma, addiction, and much more. We must ask ourselves the following: *Do I feel free or bound? Why is this so?*

- *Bondage is heavy.* Bondage feels like suffocation, being shackled, confused, fear, anxiety, hindrance, ashamed, embarrassed, addicted, slavery, bitterness and in chains. It is not where we want to live and yet many of us choose to live here.

- *Freedom is living life without limitations.* When we are free, we demonstrate joy, peace, happiness and fearlessness. We are uninhibited, running & skipping, sun on our faces, wrapped in a warm blanket, forgiving, guilt-free, soaring on wings like eagles, with figurative wind blowing through our hair. It is light, easy, enjoyable, and hope-filled.

- *In order for us to understand freedom, we must understand bondage.* As a mother, we love our children more than words can express. As they grow, there are many times we must say no. For example, Johnny wants to climb onto a cabinet to reach the cookie jar; Sarah wants to go driving with her friend who's been in a wreck twice this year. Rather than looking at these things as restrictions, look at them as being hot burners on a stove that we do not want our children to touch. We are protecting them just as God protects us because he sees things that we don't see. When God tells us no, it is to protect and because he knows best. He has infinite wisdom that we do not possess. In order to live free, we cannot perceive God's instruction as bondage or restriction, rather freedom and protection.

- *Bondage can take many forms.* Guilt. Sexual addiction or immorality. Overspending. Overeating. Fear. Comparison. Obsession. Anxiety. Worry. Unforgiveness. Offense. Bitterness. Lying. Deceit. The weight of this bondage makes life miserable. It's much harder to parent well, when the weight of our own bondage has shackled us. Our bondage can overwhelm us. Too many have lived in embarrassment and shame, but God is saying to us today, we are victorious! Do not dwell in the past. Ask for his forgiveness and forgive others. Choose freedom. (It is a daily choice, sometimes hourly.)

- *Bondage can bring a lifetime of pain.* God already knows that for whatever temporary enjoyment (drugs, alcohol, pornography, excessive spending, or sexual immorality) could offer, there will always be a lifetime of pain and bondage associated with it. Think about lying and deceit. Think about a time when we have not been honest with a parent, friend, coworker, or other. Think about how entangled the process became, how heavy we felt. How we wished we could get out of it, but likely lied to further cover our tracks. The weight of that choice was much heavier than if we had simply chosen to tell the truth from the beginning. The emotional consequences of choosing to live outside of God's will leave us in a state of confusion, unrest, and unhappiness. Gal 5:13 says, "For you have been called to live in freedom, my brothers and sisters. But don't use your freedom to satisfy your sinful nature. Instead, use your freedom to serve one another in love."

- *Forgiveness is a critical area where we must experience God's freedom.* Giving forgiveness is for our benefit. We are not granting forgiveness because it is deserved or warranted by the other party, or even because they asked for it. We give it because Christ first loved and forgave us. We give it so that we may be free of that weight. Forgiveness does not mean the offense was okay; it merely means that this event no longer dictates the rest of our lives. (See Luke 23:34: *"Father forgive them, for they know not what they do."*)

- *The biggest hurdle of forgiveness can often be our receipt of it.* While forgiving others is critical and often a difficult hurdle we must face, receiving forgiveness for our own transgressions can sometimes be even harder. The weight of our past sin and the shame and embarrassment it can bring can make it difficult to move forward and receive forgiveness from others and even from the Lord. We must be willing recipients of this gift Christ paid for. Otherwise, Satan will use it to manipulate our thinking and decision-making.

- *A second form of freedom is in acceptance of discipline.* Accepting discipline can be difficult if we do not have willing hearts that are open to growth.

Discipline and accountability are necessary for our lives. We have others who are in authority of us in various capacity, e.g. pastors, employers, law enforcement, and others. Maturity gives us the freedom to both give discipline (such as with our children) and to receive discipline when we've fallen short, such as with the Lord, a spiritual authority figure, or an employer. We cannot be above receiving correction. The Lord corrects those he loves. The pride that we sometimes exhibit where "no one can tell us what to do" is a childish way of thinking that does not display humility, order, boundaries, or growth. We must have accountability and structure. We must humble ourselves and ask the Lord to reveal his ways to us through his word and godly counsel.

- *There is great freedom in surrender.* Surrendering to authority is God's design for our lives. There is freedom in knowing God loves us enough that he will lead and guide and direct. However, he also gives us free will to make a choice, and that choice is our freedom or bondage. The weight of failing to follow the Lord's guidance leads to bondage and a life that he never intended for us to live.

Group Discussion Time: (Suggested Time: 30 minutes)
Discuss questions from this week's homework on pages 195-197.

Final thoughts: (5 minutes)
2 Cor. 5:17-18 says, "In Christ you are a new creation! Old things have passed away!" Today, begins a new day in choosing freedom. Freedom begins by understanding that we no longer want the bondage that this life offers. We no longer want to walk in heavy weight and chains of a past life, past choices, or addiction. We want the honor the Lord in word and deed and this comes in making a daily choice to walk in forgiveness and have spiritual accountability.

- **Homework Assignment for Next Meeting:** Complete Study Guide (Pgs.198-200).
- **Closing Prayer**

Ministry Leader Tips:

- Thank God for the freedom he offers us through his son Jesus Christ. This chapter was strategically placed at the end of the Bible study to end this series on a high note. God's freedom gives us the ability to live our lives in a beautiful way.

- As we go through the next two weeks' teachings, first, discuss what freedom versus bondage is. What are some bondages that we struggle with? How does it make us feel? What are some key Scriptures on freedom? Why is it important that we not only accept Christ as our Savior, but then move into fully embracing his freedom for our lives?

- Christ paid for freedom in several areas in our lives. The first is to allow us the freedom to accept forgiveness. Too often, single moms cannot forgive themselves for their past. It can be hard for them to accept Christ's love and forgiveness. Spend time talking about living a life of freedom through forgiveness then move into discussing the freedom to forgive others.

- Talk about the necessity of releasing others and not holding on to the offense. This can be particularly difficult if we are talking about an ex-husband or father of our children. We single moms must understand how important this forgiveness is for us, our freedom and for our children.

Overwhelmed Leader's Guide Meeting 12: Whom the Son Sets Free (Part II)

Food and Fellowship: (Suggested time: 30 minutes)

This time can be used for meal distribution, games, ice breakers, introduction, and opening prayer, taking care to make any new attendees feel welcome and having some fun. (Note: This can also include live worship or pre-recorded music).

- **Opening Prayer**
- **Welcome & Introductions**
- **Ice Breaker:** If you have the freedom to fly anywhere in the world, where would it be and why? What would the trip look like? What sights would you see? What sounds would you hear?

Lesson Time: (Suggested time: 30 minutes)

Lesson time will include the main points from the assigned reading for each chapter. (Note: Some chapters will be sub-divided into two lessons.) Instructors can enhance lesson time by integrating personal stories and testimonials, additional scripture references, special guest speakers, etc.

- **Pages 187-195, Whom the Son Sets Free, Part II.** The focus of today's meeting is the continuance of our discussion on various areas of freedom in our lives, including freedom over addiction, freedom not to be right, and the freedom to trust in the Lord.
- *Freedom lays the groundwork for all God has in store.* Our ability to accept and choose freedom is the foundation we build on for effective parenting, future relationships, healthy work environments, financial choices, and even future ministry opportunities to do God's work.
- *Addiction comes in many forms.* When we explore addiction, we often think of drugs and alcohol. Therefore, if we don't have a substance abuse problem, we often gloss over addiction as not problematic in our lives. However, addiction comes in many forms, including, but not limited to, substance abuse, controlling behaviors, manipulation, over-spending, over-eating, obsession with physical appearance, over-exercising, sexual addiction, and more.
- *Freedom from addiction is possible and promised.* Christ died so that we may be free in all areas, not just in one area or another, but in ALL areas. You are not

destined to always be an addict just because this has been a struggle for perhaps many years or in previous generations. It does not mean recovery and freedom in this area is easy. It does not mean that the years of choosing bondage won't take intentional and hard work to move past. 1 Corinthians 10:13 says, "The temptations in our life are no different from what others experience. God will not allow the temptation to be more than we can stand. When we are tempted, he will show us a way out so we can endure." Once we have made up our minds that we want freedom in this area, then, and only then, can we begin the process of achieving freedom over it. No one can want it for us. Begin the process through prayer, counseling, professional help, spiritual accountability, journaling, developing new hobbies, and even exercise and healthy eating. Seek help immediately and do not wait!

- *The final freedom we'll explore is the freedom to not be right.* Past hurt, trauma, pride, and arrogance can sometimes implant a strong need for us to argue and constantly be right about every area in our lives. Sometimes, this is a pursuit of control and can stem from a lack of control through childhood abuse or other trauma. Other times, it is rooted in pride and must be addressed and expelled.

- ***We do not need to right every wrong.*** Many times, a past hurt or abuse can drive a strong desire for us to be right, to constantly look for a fight with others, or to be a voice for the hurting. While working towards correcting wrongs in the world for hurting people (e.g. abuse, racism, poverty eradication, trafficking, etc.) is an admirable cause, it is important that we recognize when we are struggling with an obsession to right every wrong, particularly when this has become an attempt to self-medicate in lieu of dealing with past pain. If we find that we are extremely combative in our everyday lives or engage in a high level of social media wars or office politics, this could be an indication that we're struggling with a need to be right. This is a bondage that could have a variety of roots.

- ***Relationships are more important than being right.*** In order to maintain healthy friendships, future romantic relationships, healthy work environments, and more, it is important that we lay down our need to be right. We don't have to always have the last word, quote the right Scripture, highlight others' faults, or be right. Does it mean that we never speak up? Of course not. But we should choose to use discernment. We must do all we can to live in harmony with others. There is great freedom in laying down our need to be right. We must begin to ask ourselves why we always want to fight, why we always need to be right, and what root causes to this behavior could be. There is nothing wrong with having strong convictions; there are injustices that should anger us. Our reactions to these convictions are where our freedom comes in. We don't need a cause to fight for just for the sake of fighting for the cause, and we don't need to end every conversation in an argument.

- ***Freedom to trust in the Lord requires faith.*** In Exodus 13:17-18, we see that God led the Israelites in a roundabout way to the promised land, recognizing that they may have a desire to turn around and go back to old bondage if he didn't take them on this unique path. The Israelites had been severely mistreated through many years of bondage, yet after many years of going through the abuse, God took them to the promised land the long way because he knew that despite how bad it was for them, they would want to go back if they encountered trouble. Isn't that true of all of us today? When the going gets tough and the work of freedom becomes difficult, we sometimes want to tuck our tails and run back to bondage rather than see what wonderful things are in store for us on the other side. The key to freedom is pressing past the uncomfortable to get to the other side. Trusting in the Lord doesn't mean we have it all figured out. It means that the freedom will come when we realize we will never have it all figured out but God does. It is not our job to question him. Our job is to obey him.

- ***We are the perfect one to raise our children.*** There is freedom in understanding that we will never be the perfect mom, say the right things all the time, or have the perfect face or body shape (according to the world's standard). But we are the perfect one to raise our children because God chose us! We should continue to work hard to be the best in all areas and allow ourselves to be forgiven when we fail. That is grace, and there's great freedom in that!

Group Discussion Time: (Suggested Time: 30 minutes)
Discuss questions from this week's homework on pages pgs. 196-200.

Final thoughts: (5 minutes)
We are not the mistakes we have made.

- **Closing Prayer**

Ministry Leader Tips:

- As this curriculum comes to a close, have the participants write down three things they learned from the book. How will they make choices differently because of this new revelation? How will their parenting differ from before?
- Have each participant write a letter or journal entry on a sheet of paper detailing the 5 things that have held thing in bondage for too long. What are the areas that have caused them fear? What are the areas that have been a heavy weight to bear? How might they begin to take action toward freedom in these areas?

Printed in Great Britain
by Amazon